GOOD HOUSEKEEPING
HOME SKILLS

GOOD HOUSEKEEPING

850 *Who-Knew Life Tricks!*

HOME SKILLS

Master Your Domain with Practical Solutions to Everyday Challenges

HEARST
HOME

Home is life's headquarters.

It's the physical command center where the business of living takes shape. It's where our heart is and our hearth lies, where we bring the bacon, where we set out from and, often, where we long to return. Home is where we nurture, nest, and nourish ourselves and our families.

Much has changed since *Good Housekeeping* was founded in 1885, but our focus is still on showing people how to best care for their homes, enjoy them more and appreciate the small moments that happen there. That's why I'm so excited about *Home Skills*. It's an entire book dedicated to demonstrating how to "home" better, wherever you are and whatever "home" means to you.

This is a compendium of must-master basics with more than 850 genius ideas, DIY projects and encouraging guidance from our editors and the experts at the Good Housekeeping Institute. It will become your go-to guide for kitchen know-hows, cleaning and organization tricks, home decorating and outdoor living ideas, maintenance and repair how-tos and entertaining advice for any occasion. It has instructions on how to butterfly a chicken (page 24), declutter any space (page 66), liven up your living room (page 83), banish stubborn stains (page 62), build a thriving container garden (page 151), throw the ultimate BBQ (page 162) — and so much more! Flip through the pages for inspiration or use the detailed table of contents in each chapter to find the skill you need right when you need it. Throughout, keep an eye out for QR codes that lead to helpful video content. However you use it, *Home Skills* will make your home a little sweeter, a little neater, a little happier and a lot more fun.

Taking care of your home can be so rewarding: bringing calm, building confidence and even caring for the self. After all, a space that truly feels like home allows for big thoughts, big projects and, ultimately, big living. It lets you be the version of YOU you've always wanted to be.

So dive in and discover everything it takes to make your home look, feel and run like a dream. Living your best life just got a little easier.

Jane Francisco
Editor in chief, *Good Housekeeping*

LAB TIP Think beyond drawers when it comes to storing kitchen supplies. Hanging frequently used equipment within easy reach is a practical choice that adds visual interest to your space.

CHAPTER 1

PREP & COOK

OUTFIT YOUR KITCHEN

When it comes to cookware and tools, there are so many options. How to choose? You can whip up almost any meal with the following key items.

Pots & Pans

- Dutch oven (6-quart)
- Roasting pan (13-by-9-inch)
- Saucepans (2- and 4-quart)
- Skillets (8-, 10- and 12-inch, nonstick and cast-iron)
- Square pan (8-inch)
- Stockpot (8-quart)

Bakeware

- Cake pans (two 9-inch pans)
- Cookie sheets or jelly-roll pans (two 18- x 12- inch half sheets)
- Pie plate (glass)

Appliances, Gadgets & Tools

- Cheese grater
- Colander
- Cutting boards (one for meat, one for produce)
- Food processor
- Food scale
- Ice cube trays
- Immersion blender
- Knives (see page 11 for the only knives you'll need)
- Measuring cups (for wet and dry ingredients)
- Offset spatulas, variously sized
- Peeler (see page 36 for an awesome hack)
- Reusable food wrap
- Scissors
- Slow cooker
- Storage containers, variously sized
- Zester

LAB TIP
Use an ice cube tray to make single-serve portions of leftover pasta sauce, pesto or chopped herbs (covered in olive oil). Toss them into a hot pan for soups, pastas, sautés and more. You can also freeze wine to chill sangria, or leftover juice and coconut milk to add to smoothies and cocktails.

Know Your Knives

Pros swear by this triple threat.
So do in-the-know home cooks.

Chef's Knife

The go-to blade for chopping, slicing and dicing. With its pointed tip and hefty rear, it can handle virtually every kitchen chore — think of it as the prepping workhorse you'll use most often.

Paring Knife

This little blade is ideal for peeling potatoes, segmenting oranges, slicing mushroom caps and performing other small jobs.

Bread Knife

Its serrated blade easily cuts through crusty loaves, flaky desserts or delicate items like ripe tomatoes.

LAB TIP

Look for a knife that feels comfortable and balanced in your hand.

Western-style knives are typically heavy, with thick blades.

Japanese ones can be fragile but allow for more precise cuts.

Wide, nonslip handles encourage a good grip, while thinner ones allow for more control during use.

Chef's knives commonly have 8-inch blades; opt for a 6- or 7-inch one if you have smaller hands.

SCAN ME!

HOW TO HONE A KNIFE

MASTER YOUR KNIFE TECHNIQUE

Always use a sharp chef's knife to make your presentation stand out.

Cut a Watermelon (and Other Large Fruits and Vegetables)

Slice off both ends. Halve the melon by standing it on one cut end and slicing all the way through. To make triangles or batons, slice it lengthwise. To peel and/or cube the watermelon, slice it crosswise.

LAB TIP
Always wash produce thoroughly, even if you'll be discarding the outer layer. Bacteria lurks on skins and peels, and you don't want to drag it into your produce as you cut.

Dice Potatoes (and Other Round Fruits and Vegetables)

Trim a peeled potato on all sides so it forms a rough rectangle. Next, slice the potato lengthwise in ½-inch slices. Stack the slices on top of each other and slice again lengthwise. Cut across the slices, producing a medium dice.

LAB TIP
If you're not cooking with them immediately, submerge diced potatoes in cold water until ready to use.

Julienne Carrots (and Other Long Fruits and Vegetables)

Trim off the top and bottom of a peeled carrot. Then cut it into 2- to 3-inch lengths. Trim the rounded sides of each piece to create a rectangle shape. Cut each rectangle lengthwise into ⅛-inch slices. Stack several of the slices together and cut lengthwise again, creating thin batons called "julienne."

Julienne Basil (and Other Leafy Herbs)

Start with large, unbruised basil leaves. Wash and dry them thoroughly and stack them together like sheets of paper. Gently roll up one stack into a loose cigar shape. Using a sharp knife, slice across the roll to make very thin julienne called "chiffonade."

LAB TIP
Chopped, basil will discolor very quickly when exposed to air, so hold off prepping leafy herbs until the last minute.

Mince a Jalapeño (and Other Chile Peppers)

Note: The spicy juice of jalapenos can be almost impossible to see when left on your hands. Wear gloves to be safe, and avoid touching your face or eyes.

Start by trimming the end off the pepper. Cut pepper lengthwise. Laying the knife parallel to the pepper, gently slice along the inside of the jalapeño, removing the seeds and ribs. Next, make very fine slices down the length of the pepper. Cut across these slices to create a mince.

Mince Garlic

Begin by cutting off the root end of the garlic clove. Thinly slice the entire clove lengthwise. Finally, slice it crosswise, cutting across the layers to create a fine mince.

LAB TIP
To peel garlic, place a clove on the work surface and the flat side of a large knife on top. Press down on the knife to lightly crush the garlic; remove the peel. Or try the shaking method, which works for a whole head or a few cloves: take off the outer papery skin, place the garlic in a glass or jar and shake for 30 seconds. Repeat until all the skin has fallen off.

Chop an Onion

Cut off the stem end, then cut in half. Peel off the outer layer. Place the onion on the cutting board, cut side down. Holding the top of the onion, and keeping the knife parallel to the cutting board, make about four horizontal cuts from the stem end to the root, making sure to leave the root end intact (don't cut all the way through so the onion stays together). Make vertical cuts, making sure to keep the root end intact. Cut down perpendicularly to the other vertical cuts. The thinner you make each of the original cuts, the finer the chop will be.

Slice an Avocado

Using a sharp knife, cut around the length of the avocado and twist to separate the two halves.

Whack the knife into the stone, then twist and lift it out. Gently peel away the skin, then slice or dice. Alternatively, scoop out the flesh with a spoon.

LAB TIP
If you're only using half of the avocado, prevent browning on the other half by brushing it with lime juice, then pressing plastic wrap onto the surface before refrigerating.

LAB TIP Avoid mishaps by turning your non-knife hand into a claw. Rest your fingertips on top of and your thumb alongside whatever it is you're cutting to stabilize it. Depending on the size of the object, you can rest your wrist atop the cutting board.

SCAN ME!
HOW TO CUT A PINEAPPLE

13

STOCK YOUR PANTRY

A well-stocked pantry can see you through a storm as easily as a low-key weekend of binge-watching. Keep these staples on hand.

Canned and Jarred Staples

Beans A variety of colorful options are great for chili, pastas, taco filling, salads and bean dips. Always useful on the shelf: cannellini, black, pink, pintos and chickpeas.

Chipotle Chiles Just a spoonful adds instant smokiness and a bit of heat to your favorite dishes.

Marinara Sauce As a pasta topper, it's the fastest dinner in the pantry, but you can also use it to deglaze a pan, poach eggs or make chili.

Mixed Nuts and Nut Butters Great for snacking and sandwiches.

Olives They add richness to sautés, pastas and salsas.

Roasted Red Peppers Marinate with garlic and herbs for a bruschetta topping, or add sherry and capers to sautéed chicken, pork or fish.

Salsa Try it as a pan sauce for chicken breasts: Rub the chicken with a sprinkle of chili powder and then sauté, or use it to top white fish and bake at 400°F for 15 minutes.

LAB TIP Look for cans that don't have BPA lining, an industrial chemical used to make some plastics that can be toxic.

Tomatoes Both 14 and 28 oz sizes, whole and diced. Great for pasta sauces, soups, sautés and chili.

Tuna and Salmon Look for cans without BPA lining. Flake into pasta or salads, or mix with mayo for a classic sandwich.

Packaged Grains, Snacks and More

Biscuit Mix Top a pot pie or a chili pie; make sweet or savory muffins or pancakes.

Couscous It cooks up in 5 minutes flat.

Edamame Eat these soybeans straight out of the bag, or sprinkle on pasta and salads for some crunch.

Grits Great with eggs, but also tasty baked up into a cheesy casserole or as the perfect base for saucy shrimp.

Lentils Green or brown, these cook up in less than half an hour (with no presoaking!). Try as a warm salad with chopped vegetables, mix with leftover cooked rice for a tasty complete-protein pilaf, or start a soup.

Oats Old fashioned are the most versatile variety.

Panko Use it to coat fish, chicken, pork or zucchini for easy oven-fried anything.

Pasta Keep a variety of shapes from tiny *tubetti* for soups to spaghetti for your favorite sauce.

Polenta Precooked logs are a simple side; slice and sauté or broil with a sprinkle of cheese.

Quinoa Try red, black and white varieties. Toast it in a dry skillet until fragrant to bring out its nuttiness before cooking.

Rice Brown, basmati, long grain white, Arborio.

Liquid Condiments

Coconut Milk Simmer your favorite protein in it for an easy curry, swap for milk in a smoothie, or add to desserts.

Hot Sauce A dash or two livens up any dish, especially eggs.

Ketchup The ultimate burger topper can also be mixed with a little Worcestershire, vinegar and brown sugar to make your own BBQ sauce.

Mustard Yellow, Dijon, honey, spicy brown, coarse and German — there are many options to choose from, depending on personal preference.

Olive and Vegetable Oils Drizzle olive oil over vegetables before roasting, toss with pasta or mix with vinegar for a classic salad dressing.

Soy Sauce Douse it on vegetables or rice, or use it as the basis for a marinade.

Vinegars So many options such as red and white wine, balsamic, apple cider, rice.

Worcestershire Sauce Bring the umami to stews, stocks, braises and, of course, Bloody Marys.

LAB TIP
Store liquid condiments in upper cabinets for easy reach and measuring, away from the heat and light— think near, but not above, your stove.

Shop Your Pantry

Wondering what to eat? Look in your pantry for the items below, and you'll have a meal in minutes.

Pasta Puttanesca	Salmon Bowl	Peanutty Noodles
pasta	whole-grain instant rice	spaghetti
+	+	+
tomato sauce	canned salmon	peanut butter
+	+	+
olives	edamame	soy sauce
+	+	+
chili seasoning	hot sauce	vinegar
+	+	+
canned tuna	soy sauce	edamame

SPICE UP YOUR COOKING

Spices are generally harvested from plants that grow in tropical regions, whereas what we commonly call "herbs" tend to hail from temperate zones. Both can be aromatic, add depths of flavor and provide numerous other benefits.

Find Spices Fast

Arranging your spice rack A to Z means everything is easy to find. Or, if you're more task oriented, group herbs and spices by use. Designate one shelf for baking and include extracts, cinnamon, baking powder and baking soda. Divvy up the rest by category — one area for seeds and whole spices, another for ground spices and yet another for dried herbs. It also helps to keep labels facing outward.

Spices

- allspice
- chili powder
- cinnamon
- cloves
- coriander
- cumin
- curry powder
- fennel seeds
- ginger
- nutmeg
- peppercorns
- red pepper flakes
- smoked paprika

Dried Herbs

- dill
- oregano
- rosemary
- tarragon
- thyme

BONUS RECIPE

Toasted Spice Rub

Makes **1 cup**
Total time: **10 minutes**

Toast ¼ cup fennel seeds and 1 Tbsp. coriander seeds with 1 Tbsp. peppercorns in a small, heavy pan over medium heat, stirring constantly. When fennel turns light brown, add 1½ tsp. red pepper flakes and toss several times. Turn the mixture out onto a plate to cool immediately. (Note: Turn on the exhaust fan over your stove before toasting the spices — they may begin to smoke.)

Combine toasted spices in a blender with ¼ cup chili powder, 2 Tbsp. kosher salt and 2 Tbsp. cinnamon, and pulse until mixture is evenly ground. Store spice rub in a glass jar or tin in a cool, dry place. Use on meat or fish, in soups and even on scrambled eggs.

Solve household problems with spices

Home Deodorizer

Place some cinnamon sticks, orange peels and a few cloves in a cheesecloth. Cover with water and bring to a boil for a warming aroma throughout your home.

Microwave Freshener

To get rid of lingering smells, such as burnt microwave popcorn or fish, fill a large bowl with 1 cup water and sprinkle in your favorite spice. Microwave on High until the water boils (2–3 minutes), then let it sit inside for 10 to 15 minutes to cool down. Wipe the walls clean. See page 57 for more advice about zapping odors.

Insect Repellent

Hanging bay leaves in the pantry has been shown to prevent weevils, while burning sage and rosemary helps keep mosquitoes away when entertaining alfresco. See page 159 and page 137 for more advice about banishing bugs.

> **LAB TIP**
> Replace herbs and spices every two years at least. Buy spices you don't use frequently in smaller jars so there's less waste, and keep all spices and herbs out of direct light and away from heat sources.

SUBSTITUTE with EASE

Sometimes you don't have an ingredient on hand, or you have a guest with certain dietary needs. Here's how to tweak recipes so they work for you.

Baking Powder
1 tsp. baking powder = ½ tsp. cream of tartar + ¼ tsp. baking soda.

Butter, creamed or softened
Virgin coconut oil, which is solid at room temperature, vegetable shortening or vegan butter.

Buttermilk
1 cup buttermilk = 1 Tbsp. vinegar or lemon juice plus enough milk to equal 1 cup. Let stand 5 min. to thicken. Or use 1 cup plain yogurt.

Chocolate
1 oz unsweetened chocolate = 3 Tbsp. unsweetened cocoa powder plus 1 Tbsp. butter, margarine or oil.

Broth
1 cup chicken or beef broth = 1 bouillon cube, envelope or tsp. instant bouillon plus 1 cup boiling water.

Butter, melted
Any liquid fat — like vegetable oil, olive oil, coconut oil — can be used in a 1-to-1 replacement.

Cayenne
⅛ tsp. red pepper = 4 drops hot-pepper sauce.

Cornstarch (for thickening)
1 Tbsp. cornstarch = 2 Tbsp. flour or 2 Tbsp. quick-cooking tapioca.

Egg
1 Tbsp. ground flax or chia seeds with 3 Tbsp. water, leave to thicken for about 5 min. Or ¼ cup applesauce plus a pinch of baking powder per egg.

Heavy Cream
Coconut milk or unsweetened coconut cream.

Sour Cream
1 cup sour cream = 1 cup plain yogurt. When cooking, stabilize it with 1 egg white or 1 Tbsp. cornstarch or flour dissolved in a little cold water for every qt. of yogurt.

Vanilla Extract
Brandy, or an appropriately flavored liqueur.

Fish Sauce
1 Tbsp. fish sauce = 2 tsp. soy sauce plus 1 tsp. anchovy paste.

Milk
1 cup whole milk = ½ cup evaporated milk plus ½ cup water; nondairy milks — like almond, soy, oat, coconut — can be replaced as a 1-to-1 swap.

Sugar
1 cup light brown sugar = 1 cup granulated sugar plus 1 Tbsp. molasses or 1 cup dark brown sugar.

White Wine
Apple cider vinegar, white grape juice or apple juice.

Flour (self-rising)
1 cup self-rising flour = 1 cup all-purpose flour plus ¼ tsp. baking powder and a pinch of salt.

Powdered Sugar
1 cup powdered sugar = 1 Tbsp. cornstarch plus 1 cup granulated white sugar pulsed in a food processor.

Tomato Sauce
15 oz can tomato sauce = 6 oz can tomato paste plus 9 oz water.

Yeast
1 package active dry yeast = ½ oz yeast cake or 1 package quick-rise yeast (allow half the rising time for quick-rise).

RIPEN ANYTHING

Place the unripe fruit of your choice in a paper bag at room temperature for two to three days to enjoy your rock-hard produce sooner. As it ripens, fruit emits ethylene gas; trapping the gas in the bag will help the fruit ripen. Fruit should be good to go within a couple of days, depending on how hard it was to begin with.

BONUS RECIPE

Microwave Berry Jam

Bought too many berries? Make a jam! In a large bowl, mash 2 cups berries with ⅓ cup granulated sugar. Microwave, uncovered, on High for 10 min., stirring once. Cool completely. Makes about ¾ cup, and keeps for up to 2 weeks in the fridge.

SPEED IT UP

To speed up the ripening process, toss in an apple alongside the peaches, bananas, avocados, tomatoes or whatever you're trying to ripen. Apples have more ethylene gas than other fruits, so they tend to supercharge the whole process.

SLOW IT DOWN

If you brought home more ripe peaches than you can eat within a couple of days, or your fruit has already gotten to just the right eating ripeness, pop them in the fridge. This slows down the ripening process. It also helps already-ripe fruit stay ready to eat a bit longer. But make sure to eat the fruit within a couple of days. The cold slows down ripening but doesn't stop it altogether. And a lengthy stay in the fridge can dry fruits out.

LAB TIP Cast-iron skillets are great for braising since they can go from cooktop to oven with ease. Try this: sear bone-in, skin-on chicken thighs and then finish cooking in the oven. Remove the cooked chicken from the skillet and whip up a lemony, white wine pan sauce with artichokes.

CLEAN a CAST-IRON PAN

This durable cookware can last a lifetime, but it can't be soaked, put in the dishwasher or scrubbed with scouring pads. Here's the best way to care for it.

1 After cooking, let your pan cool completely, then pour out any drippings. Wash it lightly with mild dish soap and a stiff bristled brush, then wipe dry.

3 Turn off the heat and use a paper towel to carefully rub a few drops of vegetable oil onto the inner surface.

2 Set the pan on a hot burner for 30 seconds, or until remaining moisture starts to evaporate. A bone-dry skillet is less likely to rust.

4 After the pan cools fully, store it with a fresh paper towel on its surface to absorb any lingering wetness.

SEASON A NEW CAST-IRON PAN

Cast-iron pans that have not been pre-seasoned by the manufacturer require some care before you use them. Season-ing the cookware creates a clean surface to cook food evenly, stops your food from sticking and helps prevent rust.

1. Wash your new cookware with hot, soapy water. Dry it thoroughly.

2. Using a cloth soaked in vege-table oil, rub the entire surface of the pan, including the exterior.

3. Heat the pan upside down in a 350°F oven for 1 hour. Turn off the oven and let the cast iron cool down completely in the oven.

LAB TIP To clean cast iron without soap and water, coat the bottom with kosher salt after cooking and use a wooden spoon to scrape up food bits. Once it's cool, toss out the salt and wipe the pan with a dry paper towel.

BUTTERFLY a CHICKEN

Removing the backbone from a whole chicken (a.k.a. butterflying or spatchcocking) and then flattening the bird cuts 30 to 40 minutes off the total time. This super-simple method ensures even cooking. Follow these easy step-by-step instructions.

1 Remove the neck and giblets, and pat the chicken very dry with paper towels. Using kitchen shears, cut along one side of the backbone, then cut along the other side.

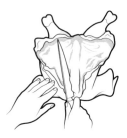

2 Flip the chicken over so the inside is facing up and—using a heavy kitchen knife—notch each side of the breastbone (this will make it easy to remove later when carving).

3 Turn the chicken back over and, holding the chicken by each breast, pull the breasts up and, with your thumbs, push the breastbone downward, to break it. Using the ball of your hand, push on the breastbone to flatten the chicken.

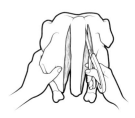

4 Fold and tuck the wing tips behind the breasts to prevent them from burning while roasting.

BONUS RECIPE
Lemon-Thyme Butterflied Roast Chicken

Serves **4**
Total time: **1 hour**

Heat oven to 425°F. On a rimmed baking sheet, toss 2 heads garlic, halved through equators, and 1 lemon, sliced, with 1 Tbsp. olive oil; toss with ¼ bunch of fresh thyme and arrange in the center of the sheet. Place the chicken on top, rub with 1 Tbsp. olive oil and season with ½ tsp. each salt and pepper. Scatter 1 lemon, cut into wedges, around it and roast 20 min. Scatter 2 cups green olives and ¼ bunch of fresh thyme around chicken and roast until chicken is golden brown and cooked through (165°F on instant-read thermometer inserted into thickest part of thigh), about 30 min. more.

COOK EGG-CELLENT EGGS

Cheap, versatile and packed with 6 grams of protein and 13 essential vitamins, eggs are one of nature's most perfect foods. Eggshell color is determined by breed — brown hens lay brown eggs, and white hens, white eggs — and has no effect on an egg's flavor or nutrition. Next time you are cooking or baking with eggs, use these clever tricks from the Test Kitchen.

Egg Separator
Thanks to the magic of suction, separating yolks from egg whites is so easy. Clean out an empty water bottle and use it to suck up the yolks from a bowl full of eggs. This only works if the yolks are intact, so be careful when cracking them to prevent bursting.

Egg Warmer
If a baking recipe calls for room-temperature eggs and you've forgotten to set some aside, just submerge eggs in a bowl of warm water for 5 minutes, drain, and use as directed.

Shell Scooper
Next time you crack eggs for scrambling and a bit of shell falls in, don't chase it with your fingers. Use another piece of shell to cut through the gloopy white and scoop it up with ease.

Perfect Peeler
After boiling eggs, drain and return to the pot. Cover with water and swirl until the shells start to crack. The rest of the shells should peel away easily. (The fresher the egg, the harder to peel.)

HARD BOILED

Place eggs in a saucepan and add water to cover by 1 inch. Bring to a boil; immediately remove from heat. Cover and let stand for desired time (see below). Transfer eggs to a bowl of ice water to cool before peeling.

4 minutes
Very runny

8 minutes
Creamy

12 minutes
Very firm, opaque

BEST-EVER SCRAMBLED EGGS

Serves **4**
Total time: **10 minutes**

In a large bowl, whisk 8 large eggs, 1 Tbsp. water and ½ tsp. each salt and pepper. Heat 1 Tbsp. olive oil or unsalted butter in a 10-inch nonstick skillet on medium. Add the eggs and cook, stirring with a rubber spatula every few seconds, to desired doneness, 2 to 3 min. for medium-soft eggs.

MIGAS

Fold 1 cup crushed tortilla chips, ¼ cup *pico de gallo* and 2 oz pepper Jack cheese (shredded) into scrambled eggs.

OLD BAY

Before scrambling, whisk 1 tsp. Old Bay Seasoning into the eggs, then scramble as directed. Fold in 1 cup cooked diced russet potato and 4 oz thinly sliced kielbasa (both browned). Sprinkle with chopped parsley.

TROUT & CRÈME FRAÎCHE

Fold ¼ cup crème fraîche, then ½ cup flaked smoked trout and ½ small red onion (thinly sliced) into scrambled eggs. Dollop with additional crème fraîche.

GRUYÈRE, BACON & SPINACH

Before scrambling, whisk 1 tsp. Dijon mustard into eggs, then scramble as directed. Fold in 2 slices of thick-cut bacon (cooked and broken into pieces) 2 cups spinach (torn) and 2 oz Gruyère (shredded).

LAB TIP

When the yolk forms, occasionally a blood vessel ruptures, causing a blood spot. These eggs are perfectly safe to eat. You can leave the red dot on the yolk or carefully remove it with the tip of a knife.

SCAN ME!

HOW TO MAKE THE BEST EGGS 8 WAYS

KEEP HERBS FRESH

Washing produce, including herbs, helps prevent soil and insect-borne illness. Storing herbs properly will make it more likely that you'll use them and cut down on food waste. For tips on growing your own herbs, see page 108.

Tender Herbs

To wash delicate herbs like basil and parsley, hold by the stems and plunge the tops into cold water. Shake to dry. After washing and drying, leave basil uncovered and store in a jar of water at room temperature. For parsley and cilantro, store them in plastic baggies or containers and keep in the fridge.

Hardy Herbs

1   For woody herbs like rosemary, thyme and oregano, swirl the sprigs around in cold water and spread them on a clean dish-towel to dry.

2   Wrap the herbs in a slightly damp paper towel. This will keep the leaves protected and hydrated, helping them stay fresh longer.

3   Store the bundles in an open plastic bag in the crisper drawer of your fridge. Check for wilted pieces every few days and replace the paper towels as needed.

Extend the Life of Your Garlic

Garlic keeps longest when stored at 60°F to 65°F and in moderate humidity. You can store garlic under an unglazed clay flowerpot in a cupboard, creating a small humidor without cutting off air circulation, which can lead to rot. Alternatively, you can try the following techniques.

Roasting It

Lightly grease a casserole dish with olive oil, chuck in some clean bulbs, and bake at 350°F until the bulbs are soft and squishy — usually about 45 minutes. Snip the tips off the bulbs and cloves, and squeeze out the incredibly tasty, and now soft, flesh. Freeze the garlic in an airtight freezer container; it'll last about a week in the fridge. The high oil content means it never freezes hard, and you can scoop the clove contents out with a spoon as needed.

Freezing It

The quickest way to prep it for freezer storage is to put the peeled cloves into a food processor or blender with a little water, pulse until they are evenly minced, and then freeze the puree in ice cube trays, or spread it out in a thin (and eventually breakable) layer on a silicone sheet. Once frozen, store the cubes or pieces in an airtight container.

Pickling It

This method mellows garlic out, making whole cloves mild enough to be tossed raw into salads or served as nibbles along with olives and such. Toss your peeled garlic cloves into a jar with some salt and vinegar and leave it in the back of your refrigerator until you run out; they'll keep indefinitely.

PREPARE BROTH

"Stock" traditionally refers to an unsalted base liquid, while "broth" is seasoned and can be sipped as is. The terms are often used interchangeably. The advantage of making your own broth? You can control the ingredients you add and make sure you're getting exactly what you want.

Chicken Broth

Serves **6**
Total time: **3 hours**

1. Place 1 small chicken (2½ to 3 lbs) in a large stockpot (this should be tall and narrow rather than short and wide) and cover with cool water (about 8 cups). Make sure to use a pot that is a few inches taller than the chicken. This allows the water to flow around the ingredients and extract the most flavor. It will also make it easier to skim away anything that rises to the surface.

2. Gently bring the water to a simmer. As it simmers, skim and discard anything that rises to the top. Simmer for 30 min.

3. Add 1 large onion, quartered (leaving the skin on is OK), 2 medium carrots, trimmed and cut into large chunks, and 2 stalks of celery, trimmed and cut into large chunks. Continue simmering for 1½ hours more.

4. Make a bouquet garni (a package of herbs wrapped in cheese-cloth): Lay 8 sprigs of parsley, 4 sprigs of thyme, 1 clove of garlic, 6 pepper-corns and 1 bay leaf on top of a folded-over piece of cheesecloth. Wrap up and tie with twine. Using this in your stock is like adding a tea bag — it will help infuse the flavor of the herbs into the broth.

5. Add the bouquet garni to the pot and simmer until the chicken is super tender and the broth is very flavorful, 30 to 45 min. (adding the herb package too early can cause the flavors to cook away completely or become dull).

6 Transfer the chicken and vegetables to a large bowl and season the broth with salt. Shred the meat, discarding the skin and bones, and reserve to serve with soup or use for another recipe.

7 Line a colander with rinsed cheesecloth (set over another pot or measuring cup), and ladle the broth into it. This will catch any additional scraps left in the broth.

8 Transfer broth to jars or containers. Refrigerate for up to 5 days or freeze for up to 3 months.

Make a Delicious Vegetable Broth

Combine 4 large leeks, thinly sliced, with 1 clove of garlic, 1 cup water, and a pinch of salt, then simmer over medium heat, covered, until leeks are tender, about 15 min. Add 1 large potato, peeled and diced; 1 small fennel bulb, trimmed and chopped; 3 parsnips, peeled and diced; 2 large carrots, peeled and sliced; 3 stalks of celery, sliced; 4 oz mushrooms, trimmed and sliced; 10 fresh sprigs of parsley; 4 sprigs of thyme; 2 bay leaves; 1 tsp. whole black peppercorns; and 12 cups water. Heat to boiling, then reduce heat and simmer, uncovered, for 1 hr. and 30 min. Season with salt and pepper, then strain the broth through a fine-mesh sieve into containers, pressing on the vegetables with the back of a wooden spoon to extract as much liquid as possible; cool. Cover and refrigerate for up to 3 days, or freeze for up to 4 months.

MAKE a GREAT CUP of COFFEE

Using fresh, whole coffee beans makes a big difference. Grind them well to the optimal size and consistency for the specific method. Use a digital scale to measure your ground coffee for precise results.

Cold Brew

Cold brew coffee is made by soaking coarse-ground coffee beans in cold or room-temperature water for 12 hours or more, and then filtering out the grounds. The result is a coffee concentrate, which can be served with water or milk.

How to make it: Add coarse-ground coffee and water to a jar or a cold brew maker. Give it a good stir before storing it in the refrigerator or at room temperature, allowing it to steep for at least 12 hours. Strain into a clean vessel, using a mesh filter lined with a coffee filter or a cheesecloth. Store in the refrigerator.

Type of grind: Coarse

Ground coffee to water ratio (in grams): 1:12

Brewing time: 12 hrs.

Resulting brew: Smooth, mellow

Pour-Over

One of the oldest ways to brew coffee, this method involves pouring hot water through coffee grounds placed in a filter to allow the coffee to drip slowly.

How to make it: Place a filter in a coffee cone dripper over a cup or carafe. Rinse the filter with hot water (to seal the filter in place), then discard the water. Add fine coffee grounds into the filter before pouring enough boiling water over them to saturate the grounds fully, waiting for 30 seconds to allow the grounds to "bloom." Then continue to pour the water in a circular motion until you reach your desired final brew weight.

Type of grind: Fine to medium

Ground coffee to water ratio (in grams): 1:16

Brewing time: 3 to 4 minutes

Resulting brew: Nuanced, smooth

BREW a PERFECT CUPPA

Follow these steps to brewing tea, from start to finish.

1 **Splurge.** Buy high-quality loose-leaf teas or tea bags for premium taste. Measure out 1 tsp. of leaves per 6 oz cup.

2 **Use a teapot for steeping.** It retains heat better to bring out flavor. Swirl hot water in the pot to preheat for steeping at the correct temperature.

3 **Pour, don't dunk.** Pour water over leaves (instead of adding water first) to boost taste and get more antioxidants.

4 **Give it a minute.** Tea needs time to steep.

TEA	MINUTES	TEMP (°F)
Black	3 to 5	201° to 210°
Chinese Green	1 to 3	170° to 180°
Darjeeling	3	190° to 195°
Japanese Green	1 to 2	160° to 175°
Oolong	3 to 5	175° to 195°
White	3 to 4	185°

COOK SMARTER

This handy chart shows exactly how many of what goes into how many of which, so you can easily switch up your recipes.

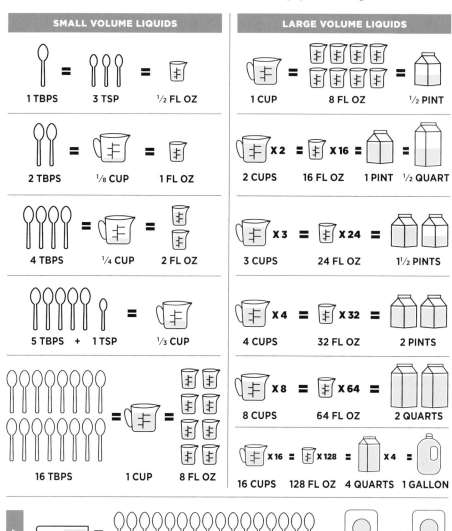

SMALL VOLUME LIQUIDS		
1 TBPS	3 TSP	½ FL OZ
2 TBPS	⅛ CUP	1 FL OZ
4 TBPS	¼ CUP	2 FL OZ
5 TBPS + 1 TSP		⅓ CUP
16 TBPS	1 CUP	8 FL OZ

LARGE VOLUME LIQUIDS		
1 CUP	8 FL OZ	½ PINT
2 CUPS	16 FL OZ	1 PINT — ½ QUART
3 CUPS	24 FL OZ	1½ PINTS
4 CUPS	32 FL OZ	2 PINTS
8 CUPS	64 FL OZ	2 QUARTS
16 CUPS	128 FL OZ	4 QUARTS — 1 GALLON

DRY

1 CUP	16 TBPS	1 LB	16 OZ

MEASURE PRECISELY

When it comes to baking, recipes depend on the correct ratio of ingredients — plus chemistry — to work. Follow these guidelines when prepping ingredients to make sure your final product has the right taste and texture.

For liquids, use a clear measuring cup with a spout. Place it on a flat surface and add the desired amount of liquid. Bend down to check the accuracy; don't try to gauge from above.

For dry ingredients, spoon and sweep the ingredient into flat-topped measuring cups. When measuring flour, stir it with a fork or whisk to aerate it before spooning. Overfill the cup slightly and then use a straight-edge to level it off. Don't scoop the cup directly into the flour; you'll pack it down, and the result will be a drier baked good.

Brown sugar, butter and shortening — unlike flour — should be firmly packed into the cup and hold its shape when turned out.

When measuring sticky ingredients like molasses, honey or syrup, lightly grease the cup with vegetable oil or cooking spray first. The ingredient will slide out, leaving none behind.

LAB TIP Liquid measuring cups are designed with handles and pour spouts, while dry measuring cups are best for ingredients like flour and sugar as you can fill the cups and level them off without inadvertently packing the dry ingredient down. It's best to use measuring cups for their intended purpose to get the most accurate (and mess-free!) results.

BAKE BETTER

Ready for some genius hacks to make your baked goods even more delicious (and even professional looking)?

Measuring Matters

Measure dry and wet ingredients in their respective cups. (Dry measuring cups are the ones that nest inside each other. Liquid measuring cups are the ones with spouts and are only used for liquids.) See page 35 for best practices while measuring.

One Pan at a Time

For best results, bake only one pan in your oven at a time. If you do use two, be sure the oven racks are spaced apart and then rotate the cookie sheets between racks halfway through the baking time.

Quick Room-Temperature Butter

Warm cold butter quickly by carefully filling a glass with hot water and letting it sit for a moment. Then pour the water out and invert the glass over the stick of butter. Five minutes later, you'll have room-temperature butter.

Use a Vegetable Peeler for Chocolate Curls

To decorate your cakes and cupcakes with fancy chocolate curls, grab the vegetable peeler. Run it alongside a bar of chocolate to create delicate little swirls.

Be a Little Salty

It might sound counterintuitive, but sprinkling cookies with finishing salt creates a more complex flavor. Salt helps you to better taste the intense sweetness of sugar.

LAB TIP For recipes that don't specify which to use, go with the butter — salted or unsalted — that will most suit your palate. If you're baking a recipe that calls for unsalted butter (or doesn't specify a butter) and you only have salted on hand, just eliminate any added salt in the recipe.

PREP A PIECRUST

Master rolling and shaping for a flawless pie every time.

Roll the chilled dough into a 12-inch circle on a floured surface with a floured pin.

Fold dough over the pin, transfer to a pie plate and unfold dough.

Fit into the bottom and up the sides, then trim so the overhang is even all the way around.

Fold overhang under to create a thicker rim of dough, then crimp.

Frost a Cake Like a Pro

1. **Trim and stack your cake layers** (with whatever filling you're using), and crumb-coat the whole thing. Crumb-coating involves applying a very thin layer of frosting to prevent your cake from crumbling. It's like primer when painting; it prevents imperfections from coming through.

2. **Transfer the stacked cake** to a cardboard cake circle the same diameter as (or slightly larger than) the cake.

3. **Frost just the top** of the cake.

4. **Press another cake circle** (same size as the bottom one) into the frosting on top of the cake so you have one solid cylinder with cardboard on both ends, creating a slight overhang. Freeze until the frosting is very firm — this will help the circle peel off easily.

5. **Generously press and smooth** the remaining room-temperature frosting around the sides of the cake using a large offset spatula and the cardboard edges as your guide.

6. **Try doing swoops and swirls** in the frosting with the end of a mini offset spatula for a professional look. Or cover your cake in colorful cereal, candy, sprinkles or fruit leather cut into fun shapes.

FREEZE EVERYTHING

Move over ice cream, it's time for some company. Follow the manufacturer's instructions or use the following recommended times.

Dairy

Ice cream
3-4 months

Salted butter
3-4 months

Unsalted butter
6-8 months

Fruit

Fruit in syrup
9-12 months

Fruit juice
4-6 months

Fruit purees
6-8 months

Whole fruit
6-8 months

Meat

Beef or veal
4-6 months

Chicken/turkey
4-6 months

Cured meat
2-3 months

Duck/goose
4-6 months

Ham/bacon joints
3-4 months

Lamb
4-6 months

Pork
4-6 months

Sliced bacon
2-3 months

Prepared Foods

Bread
4-6 months

Bread dough
2-3 months

Cakes
4-6 months

Pastries
2-3 months

Prepared meals
4-6 months

Soups and sauces
3 months

Stocks: 6 months

Sandwiches
2-3 months

Fish

Fish portions
3-4 months

Oily fish
3-4 months

Shellfish
2-3 months

Whole fish
6-8 months

Vegetables

Blanched vegetables
10-12 months

Tomatoes
6-8 months

Unblanched vegetables
3-4 months

Vegetable purees
6-8 months

LAB TIP You don't have to thaw frozen bread. When you're ready to eat, simply unwrap the frozen slice and pop it in the toaster or under the broiler.

PRESERVE FRESH PRODUCE

If you've overbought at the grocery store and you know that you won't be able to use up fruit or vegetables before they start to spoil, a good way to prolong their life is to freeze them.

Berries are particularly good candidates for freezing.

Stem or hull them, halve them if they're large, and freeze them in a single layer on a parchment-lined rimmed baking sheet until firm. Then transfer them to freezer-safe containers or plastic freezer bags.

To freeze vegetables, blanch them first.

Cook them in rapidly boiling salted water for the recommended time or until just tender. Then cool them quickly in an ice-water bath and drain well. This slows or stops the action of enzymes that can cause loss of flavor, color and texture. Freeze them on baking sheets just like you did the berries, and then transfer to containers and return to the freezer. Cook frozen vegetables with or without thawing.

DEFROST MEAT FAST

The best and safest way to defrost meat is overnight in the refrigerator, until it is completely thawed. After thawing, ground meat, poultry and seafood should keep well in the refrigerator for a day or two, while red meat (beef, pork, lamb and steak) stays good for 3 to 5 days. Plus, if you thaw meat in the refrigerator, you can freeze it again safely.

However, you don't have to thaw frozen meat before cooking. It's safe to cook fresh-out-of-the-freezer blocks of ground turkey, solid cuts of chicken and bricks of ice-cold steak. The meat will take longer to cook (about 50% more time), and it's not ideal for achieving golden-crispy skin or a perfect sear. Instead, toss it in soups or stews.

REDUCE FOOD WASTE

It's easy to reduce your environmental footprint while saving money — here's how.

Beware of bulk.

Only stock up on items that can be safely stored for the long haul. Think seafood, nuts and seeds, which can last up to a year in the freezer. Crackers, cereals and dried beans will stay fresh if they're stored in a cool, dry pantry and not exposed to sunlight.

Rotate items on your shelf.

When you buy new food from the store, bring all the older items in your cupboards and fridge to the front. By putting the old stuff in sight, you run less risk of finding something moldy in the back.

Try pickling.

Making homemade pickles is our favorite way to preserve vegetables. Try our go-to brine with carrots, green beans, cucumbers or zucchini:

In a small pot, mix $1^1/_4$ cups distilled white vinegar; 1 cup water; 4 cloves of garlic, crushed and peeled; 3 Tbsp. sugar; and 2 Tbsp. kosher salt. Heat on medium, stirring, until sugar dissolves. Arrange 1 lb desired vegetables, quartered lengthwise, and 3 sprigs of dill in a 32 oz jar; pour warm brine over vegetables to cover. Let cool slightly. Replace lid and refrigerate at least 4 hours or up to 2 weeks.

Compost.

It's one of the most effective ways to minimize the amount of garbage your family sends to the landfill. Not only does this reduce methane gas (a major factor in global warming), but it also controls trash odor and gives you rich fertilizer. See our tips on page 161 for starting your own composting bin.

Rethink "expiration dates."

Food does not generally have an expiration date, but will have a "use by" and/or "sell by" date. "Use by" indicates optimal freshness, and "sell by" is a guideline for retailers on how long to display it. Proper storage is key (below 41°F for anything refrigerated; below 0°F for anything frozen). Questioning whether a food may make you sick? Better to toss it than take a risk.

BONUS RECIPE
No-Waste Pesto

Rather than tossing carrot tops, radish leaves or beet greens, make an easy pesto: In a food processor, combine 2 cups rinsed carrot tops (tough stems removed), $^1/_2$ cup basil, $^1/_2$ cup grated Parmesan, $^1/_3$ cup toasted almonds, 1 small clove of garlic, $^1/_2$ tsp. salt and $^1/_4$ tsp. pepper. Pulse to finely chop. Drizzle in $^3/_4$ cup olive oil. Serve over cooked noodles or as a tasty dip.

LAB TIP
Looking for a quick, satisfying, endlessly customizable dinner that will help you use up leftovers? Preheat your oven to 450°F. On a sheet pan, combine vegetables and proteins of your choice with olive oil, salt, and spices (like cumin and smoked paprika) and roast them for 20 to 35 min until the protein is cooked and the vegetables are soft.

LAB TIP Don't forget to clean your cleaning supplies! Frequently sanitizing scrub brushes and sponges ensures that you don't inadvertently spread bacteria while you tidy.

CHAPTER 2

CLEAN & ORGANIZE

Know When to Clean Everything

This super-handy checklist will help you stay on top of how often to break out your cleaning supplies — it's less than you think!

EVERY DAY

- [ ] Clean coffee maker
- [ ] Clean dirty dishes
- [ ] Do laundry as needed
- [ ] Make bed
- [ ] Sanitize kitchen & bathroom sinks
- [ ] Squeegee shower walls
- [ ] Sweep kitchen floors
- [ ] Wipe down bathroom surfaces
- [ ] Wipe down kitchen counters & table

EVERY WEEK

- [ ] Change bedding
- [ ] Clean microwave
- [ ] Clean mirrors
- [ ] Dust furniture
- [ ] Mop kitchen & bathroom floors
- [ ] Sanitize sponges
- [ ] Scrub bathroom surfaces
- [ ] Toss expired food
- [ ] Vacuum floors & furniture
- [ ] Wipe down kitchen appliances

EVERY MONTH

- [ ] Dust & clean light fixtures
- [ ] Dust blinds
- [ ] Clean dishwasher, laundry machines & vacuum
- [ ] Vacuum vents & woodwork

EVERY 3-6 MONTHS

- [ ] Clean out freezer
- [ ] Clean range hood
- [ ] Clean patio surfaces & furniture
- [ ] Clean under & behind furniture
- [ ] Descale coffee maker
- [ ] Freshen drains & disposal
- [ ] Vacuum mattress
- [ ] Wash car
- [ ] Wash pillows & comforters
- [ ] Wash shower-curtain liner
- [ ] Wipe down inside of fridge

EVERY YEAR

- [ ] Clean around dryer & vents
- [ ] Clean chimney & fireplace
- [ ] Clean drapes & curtains
- [ ] Clear out gutters
- [ ] Deep clean carpet & upholstery
- [ ] Deep clean windows

LEARN from EXPERT CLEANERS

Professional cleaners have seen it all. So you can rest assured that their helpful hacks can conquer any mess — and keep little messes from turning into big ones.

Think of everything as a grid.
Whether it's a mirror, a countertop or an entire floor, visualizing it as a grid means you won't miss a spot or clean any area twice.

Work from top to bottom.
Always do your floors last. That way you're not shaking dust and dirt onto any surface you've already cleaned.

Have "house only" shoes.
Taking shoes off at the door helps keep dirt outside. Designate a pair of slippers or sneakers as your indoor shoes.

Use cooking downtime.
Don't waste time watching that pot boil. As food cooks, wipe counters, rinse prep tools and put stuff away.

Stash cleaning tools nearby.
Busy rooms get dirty fast, but with cloths, dusters, a lint roller or even a handheld stick vac handy, it will be easy to zap dust, blot spills or pick up pet hair when you see it.

Deal with clothing as soon as you take it off.
Whether you hang it, add it to the laundry bin or fold it, never let anything land on the floor.

Freshen fabrics.
Give decorative pillows and throws a tumble in the dryer on the air-only cycle to fluff them and remove loose dust. Pass a garment steamer over upholstery to release odors and kill dust mites.

Vacuum first, then mop.
When mopping, start from the far corner and work toward the door.

Finish with the bathroom.
To lower bacteria transfer, start your chores in the bedroom, then move to high-germ zones like the kitchen and bathroom.

SCAN ME!
6 CLEANING SECRETS TO BORROW FROM HOTEL CLEANING STAFF

SPEED-CLEAN EVERY ROOM

In as little as 60 seconds, you can tidy messes all over the house. Here's what to tackle when time is ticking.

Tidy a junk drawer.

Take out what doesn't belong and stash it elsewhere. Suck up crumbs and dust with your hand vac's crevice tool. Straighten the rest.

Vacuum doormats.

Vacuum the top, flip it over, then vacuum the back to push deeply embedded dirt out onto the floor, where it's easy to pick up.

Make glass doors gleam.

Remove prints and pet smudges from front, back and patio door glass with a spray and a micro-fiber cloth. Or just wet half the cloth to spot-clean and use the other half to dry.

Tackle the trash can.

Go over the lid, sides, front and foot pedal (if there is one) with a sanitiz-ing wipe or a damp cloth or paper towel to remove drips and dried food bits and help nix odors. Toss the trash and put in a fresh liner.

Spruce up the bathroom.

It's possible to give your bathroom a quick sanitizing without a top-to-bottom cleaning. Use a germ-killing wipe or spray on the hot spots, like the faucet, flush handle and toilet seat. Keep surfaces wet for the time stated on the label. While waiting, straighten the sink area and put out clean towels. And see page 49 for advice about keep-ing your bathroom clean for longer.

Dust ceiling fans.

If you have an extendable duster, now is the time to use it. Go over both sides of the blades, the motor and any lights. Or use your vacuum's extension wands and dusting brush to reach what you can.

Focus on wood floors.

Dust and grit are a wood floor's worst enemies. Ground in, they can scratch and dull the finish. Quick cleanings with a dry mop or a vacuum made for wood floors are your best defense.

Unclog the clothes dryer.

Excess lint in and around this appliance is a fire hazard, and cleaning just the filter screen isn't enough. Remove the lint filter and, with a brush or your vacuum's crevice tool, clean as far into the slot as you can reach. With a flat duster or a sock attached to a broom handle, pull dust clumps from underneath and around the dryer.

IN 30 MINUTES, YOU CAN

Clean out the fridge.

No need to do a full-on emptying. Toss expired and spoiled foods. Move items on a shelf to one side and wipe the open space with a warm, sudsy cloth. Rinse and do the same for the other half. Repeat with the remaining shelves and bins. Don't forget the door.

Zap mildew stains.

Attack moldy grout when you see it so weekly bathroom cleanings will be faster and easier. Spritz grout cleaner or a mix of one part chlorine bleach and two or three parts water on just the stains. Let set a few minutes. Scrub with a stiff, narrow brush, then rinse with a wet sponge or cloth. See page 131 for more mold-busting tips.

Freshen sheer curtains.

Take down sheers and tumble them in the dryer in a 10-minute air-only cycle to help eliminate dust and odors. Remove them promptly from the dryer and rehang them to help any creases fall out.

Deodorize fabrics.

Sprinkle baking soda or a carpet-freshening powder on rugs, pet beds and upholstery to remove stale odors. See page 52 for baking soda instructions.

IN 1 HOUR, YOU CAN

Revive a mattress.

Strip the bed and steam the surface with a garment steamer or an iron to release odors and kill dust mites. With your vacuum's upholstery and crevice tools, go over the top and sides, pressing down on the fabric and into the quilting and along the edges. Spray with a fabric sanitizer and let air-dry.

Degrease the kitchen.

Kitchen dust is greasy dust, and it builds up on cabinets, countertop appliances, the fridge and light fixtures without your even seeing it. To minimize scrubbing, clean them with a spray that dissolves grease on contact; pick one that's safe for a variety of surfaces.

Wash and dry pillows.

In just 1 hour, you can machine-wash and dry synthetic-fiber-filled bed pillows. Choose a short, gentle cycle; add a second rinse; and tumble dry on medium. Washing two at a time will help balance the load.

Perk up the patio or deck.

Brush loose dust and spiderwebs from benches, tables and chairs. Spot-clean or wash with a sudsy cloth, a furniture cleaner or baking soda (see page 52 for instructions). Hose off to rinse and let air-dry.

GET READY for **GUESTS—FAST**

You just found out that your parents or in-laws are on their way. Here's how to clean up *fast*.

1 Start with the bathroom.
Use an all-purpose disinfecting wipe to clean the sink, counter and toilet top. Wipe down the mirror and fixtures, straighten the shower curtain and hang fresh towels.

2 Move on to the kitchen.
Hide dirty dishes and cookware in the dishwasher if it's empty; if not, hide them in the oven. Wipe counters.

3 Declutter living spaces.
Put newspapers, magazines, shoes, clothes and whatever else is lying around into a shopping bag or laundry basket, then hide the bag or basket in a bedroom or a closet.

4 End with the floors.
Vacuum main areas and living spaces, including carpets and bare floors. Store the vacuum in the closet, and greet your guests.

KEEP YOUR BATHROOM CLEAN for LONGER

Freshen up the place where you freshen up.

1 Squeegee your shower. Nothing helps delay mildew stains like a dry shower. Hang a squeegee from the showerhead, and make it a rule that the last one to take a shower wipes down the walls, tub and shower doors. A couple of extra minutes of work can minimize cleaning time in the long run.

2 Wipe up toothpaste splatters, water marks and other messes when you see them so they don't have a chance to dry and become tougher to remove.

3 Combat shower-curtain buildup. Spritz the bottom of a vinyl shower-curtain liner several times a month with a bleach-containing all-purpose or bathroom cleaner to keep soap scum, water minerals and mildew at bay. Just let the shower rinse it off (before you hop in) and you won't need to launder the curtain as often.

4 Maintain order. Dedicate spots for cosmetics and hair tools so they can be stashed away but remain within reach. Shed packaging, and store products in jars and baskets. A clutter-free counter instantly makes a bathroom look and feel cleaner.

5 Install ample towel bars. Towels will dry more quickly, and your bathroom will look tidier when you hang them where they can air-dry. No wall space? Consider an over-the-door towel bar.

6 Coat shower walls and doors with a water repellent. Doing so helps water, minerals and soap scum bead up and run off, so there's less for you to scrub away.

7 Skip bar soap at the sink. Use a liquid soap with a pump or even a hands-free soap dispenser instead. Eliminating the grimy soap dish will help your sink and countertop stay goop-free.

WASH YOUR SHOWER CURTAIN

Opening a window and turning on the exhaust fan while showering, and leaving the bathroom door open after you're done, will help moisture dissipate and prevent mold. Washing your shower curtain every three to six months will help as well.

Plastic or vinyl
Wash the curtain on the highest water level with detergent. Add two to three bath towels for extra cleaning agitation, then hang it to dry or put it in the dryer on low heat or fluff only.

Fabric
This may include cotton, nylon, polyester or hemp materials. If your shower curtain is made of one of these fabrics, or is decorative, follow the instructions on its care label.

TIDY UP AFTER PETS

Four-legged friends bring so much joy, love and, yes, messes into our lives.

Remove fur from floors.

Spritz carpeting with antistatic spray. Set your vacuum's rotating brush to the highest level that still skims the carpet, and go over the trail your pet has left. For furry tufts on bare floors, use a dry sweeper. In a rush? Scoop up clumps in corners and around furniture legs with a damp paper towel or micro- fiber cloth.

If your pet brings in mud, fight the urge to scrub the spots right away: Mud will be easier to vacuum away when dry. Blot whatever remains with dish liquid mixed with warm water.

Fight smells.

Deodorize soft places (including the dog bed) by sprinkling surfaces with baking soda (see page 52 for instructions). Scoop kitty's clumps out of the litter box and shake baking soda over the remaining litter.

Stop stains.

To get rid of accidents on carpet or upholstery — and the smells that pets keep revisiting — mix 1 cup water and $1/8$ tsp. dish soap, and blot the mess with a clean cloth. Then wash out the soap by dabbing it with 1 Tbsp. white vinegar mixed with 1 cup water. For tile stains, rub the spot with a paste made of baking soda and a little water.

To clean feces, mix 1 Tbsp. dish soap, 1 Tbsp. white vinegar and 2 cups warm water. Blot the stain with the mixture until it disappears. If it persists, use an eyedropper to add a few drops of hydrogen peroxide, and then add a drop or two of ammonia. Dab with water.

LAB TIP Lessen sofa odor by slipping dryer sheets into envelopes and tucking them under the cushions.

Organize their food.

If dry food keeps spilling, repackage it in a jumbo plastic container with a lid. If you're concerned about ants getting into pet food, flip the bowl upside down and dab some petroleum jelly near the base. Ants won't be able to climb over it to approach the food.

Collect fur on furniture.

The reason fur clings to upholstery: static electricity. Liberally spray furniture with an antistatic spray. Then put on a clean pair of rubber gloves, lightly dampen them with water and run gloved hands over cushions (for silk, use dry gloves). Or, after you're through washing dishes, don't remove your damp gloves — take a detour through the living room and quickly pick up errant fur. Wipe hair clumps from the gloves with a moist towel.

SOLVE PROBLEMS
with BAKING SODA

Sure, it's great for cookies, but its real claim to fame is the power to freshen and clean.

Dirty Patio Furniture

Before you set out your lawn chairs, scrub them with a mixture of $\frac{1}{4}$ cup baking soda and 1 qt. water, and then rinse off and let dry. And before you put them away at the end of the summer, place baking soda underneath the cushions or inside their storage bags to help keep them fresh.

Dirty Sneakers

Mix up a thin paste of 1 Tbsp. baking soda and $\frac{1}{2}$ Tbsp. each of hydrogen peroxide and warm water. Dip an old toothbrush or soft brush into the baking soda / peroxide paste and gently scrub your shoes. The hydrogen peroxide acts like an all-fabric bleach to whiten the canvas fabric, and the baking soda helps scrub away scuffs and stains. Thoroughly wipe your sneakers with a clean wet cloth to remove all the cleaning paste and soil.

Musty Carpet and Upholstery

Deodorize the soft, cushy places around your house (including pet beds) with a sprinkling of baking soda. Work the baking soda into deep-pile carpets with your fingers. Allow to sit for a few hours or overnight, then vacuum.

Greasy Pans and Dishes

Give baked-on food the one-two punch by dialing up your dish detergent's power with a sprinkling of baking soda.

Grimy Fruits and Vegetables

Mixed with water, baking soda can take off dirt and the waxy coating on produce. Use 1 tsp. baking soda for every 2 cups of water for 12 to 15 minutes. You can scrub firm produce with a brush and clean delicate ones with your hands.

Grungy Bath Toys

Fight the effects of grubby hands by wiping toys with a sponge dipped in a mixture of $\frac{1}{4}$ cup baking soda and 1 qt. water.

Kitchen Messes and Smells

Use baking soda with water to wipe countertops, microwaves and cooking utensils. Pour baking soda straight from the box and into your drain or garbage disposal to remove odors, or use in your fridge to prevent lingering food smells (see page 57 for more info).

MAKE YOUR OWN CLEANERS

These DIY products will kick grime to the curb and keep your wallet happy.

Scented All-Purpose Cleaner

Combine one part white vinegar, one part water, lemon rind and rosemary sprigs, pour into a spray bottle, shake and then let it infuse for a week before using. Use it to remove hard-water stains, clean trash cans, wipe away wall smudges and more.

LAB TIP Never use vinegar, lemon or any other acidic cleaner on marble or granite surfaces, as they will etch into the stone.

Mild Marble Cleaner

Squirt 2 drops of mild dish soap into 2 cups warm water to clean natural stone countertops. Sponge over marble and rinse completely to remove any soap residue. Buff with a soft cloth; do not let the marble air-dry.

Heavy-Duty Scrub

Rust stains on porcelain or enamel sinks and tubs are no match for this cleaner. Dip $1/2$ lemon into $1/2$ cup borax powder and scrub the surface, then rinse. (This is not safe for marble or granite.)

DIY Glass Cleaner

Combine 2 cups water, $1/2$ cup white or cider vinegar, $1/4$ cup rubbing alcohol 70% concentration and 1 to 2 drops of orange essential oil for smell (optional). Pour mixture into a spray bottle.

Clothing Stain Remover

Treat stained but washable white clothing by mixing 1 gallon hot water, 1 cup powdered dishwasher detergent and 1 cup regular liquid chlorine bleach (not ultra or concentrate) in a stainless steel, plastic or enamel basin (not aluminum). Soak garment for 15 to 20 min, then wash the item as usual. See page 62 for more info about dealing with stains.

LAB TIP Do not combine ammonia-based cleaners with chlorine bleach or products containing bleach, such as powdered dishwasher detergent. The fumes they'll create are extremely dangerous. Always label any bottles of DIY cleaners with all the ingredients inside. In case a child or animal gets into it, it's important to know what the mixture contains.

FOOLPROOF YOUR FRIDGE

Stash foods in the right place, and they'll stay freshest and last longer.

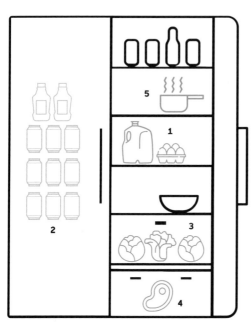

LAB TIP The doors always fluctuate the most (some chill is lost every time you open them!), so they're a no-go zone for perishables.

TIDY YOUR FRIDGE

1. Take everything out, including shelves and bins. Wipe dried food from any bottles. Toss perishable foods that are past their prime.

2. Wash shelves and bins with warm, soapy water and a sponge; air-dry. Fill a bucket with more soapy water; sponge the inside and wipe the gasket around the door. For glued-on gunk, soak a paper towel in hot water and place on crud for a few minutes to soften; wipe and toss. Dry with a soft cloth. Reinsert shelves.

3. Put everything back. Move perishables to the front so you'll eat them before they spoil.

1 **Dairy and Eggs**
Keep on interior shelves where temperatures are highest.

2 **Soft Drinks and Condiments**
Nonperishables can be kept in door compartments.

3 **Leafy Greens and Fruit**
Set in your bottom bins or drawers.

4 **Meat and Cold Cuts**
Stash in temperature-controlled drawers on the lowest setting.

5 **Warm Leftovers or Hot Soup**
Heat rises, so keep these foods on the top shelf.

SCAN ME!
HOW TO ORGANIZE YOUR FRIDGE

CLEAN CABINETS and DECLUTTER DRAWERS

Organize your kitchen so it stays that way — once and for all!

1 Work on a single cabinet at a time.
Pull everything out, clean the shelves and make sure everything that goes back inside is near where it will be used (cereal near the breakfast table, pots near the stove, spices near a food-prep counter).

2 Think small on top, big below.
Store larger items like mixing bowls, waffle irons and baking trays in under-counter cabinets. Whenever possible, nest your pots (store one inside another) to reduce the space they take up. Consider investing in a slide-out cabinet tray, which can tuck away behind cabinet doors, or hang pots and pans with handles/loops.

3 Keep frequently used items within easy reach.
Stow dishware and glasses on an accessible shelf in a cupboard close to where you usually eat. Store glasses in rows so it's easy to see where they belong, and to prevent breakage, don't crowd them.

4 Keep like with like.
Organize by type of item to keep drawers neat and tidy. Don't keep serving spoons and wine openers with things like notepads, pencils and takeout menus.

5 Store large utensils separately.
Consider using a pretty holder beside the stove.

6 Bring a few office supplies into the kitchen.
Use plastic letter trays (they'll stand up to moisture) to stack unruly packages of meat and bags of vegetables in the freezer. In the pantry and the fridge, enlist bright-colored bins for items that are near spoiling or close to their "use by" dates.

REFRESH STAINLESS STEEL APPLIANCES

Bye-bye grease stains, fingerprints and smudges.

CLEAN YOUR RANGE HOOD

1. Remove only the large metal mesh filter (the part that gets the gunkiest), and swish it in a sink filled with warm water and dish soap.

2. Dip a cloth in the same soapy water, and clean the exterior surface only (including the lightbulb, if exposed) and knobs and switches.

3. Rinse everything you just wiped down with a cloth dipped in clear water. Carefully replace the mesh filter once it's totally dry.

Grab your glass-and-surface cleaner.
Wet a soft microfiber cloth. Lightly spritz handles and areas where you see the most smudges.

Wipe in one direction.
Go with the metal's grain, adding more cleaner if needed. Target areas behind the handles and around knobs. Avoid wiping in circles, as this will cause streaking. Buff with a clean part of the cloth.

Rub with mineral oil.
With a paper towel, apply a thin coat of mineral oil to the surfaces you're cleaning — it will help minimize future fingerprints if your cleaner doesn't already have a protectant built into the formula.

ZAP KITCHEN ODORS

Because the lingering scent of last night's broiled fish is just not appetizing.

Combat cooking fumes.

In a saucepan, mix 3 Tbsp. white vinegar and 1 cup water; boil for several minutes. Vinegar is acidic and odors are alkaline, so the former will neutralize the latter.

LAB TIP After slicing onions or mincing garlic, neutralize smelly hands by rubbing fingers on a stainless steel spoon under running water.

Freshen up the fridge.

Empty the fridge, toss past-their-prime leftovers and other likely offenders and dump the old ice cubes, which hold odors,

in the sink. Clean obvious spills with a sudsy sponge; rinse. Pour a thin (¼-inch) layer of fresh baking soda into a few small, shallow dishes. Cover with plastic wrap and punch holes so air can circulate; distribute on shelves to freshen for up to 3 months. You can also store an open box of baking soda in the fridge.

Clean the dishwasher.

Remove food particles from the filter (below the bottom rack) with a paper towel. Then run a Rinse Only or Quick Rinse cycle with the machine empty, to wash away debris; afterward, leave the door a bit ajar to air it out.

Rinse the sink.

The culprit here is residual food scraps in the garbage disposal or pipes. First, clean the disposal blades by grinding up ice from the freezer. Thoroughly rinse the rubber gasket, if you have one — it's a magnet for debris (flip it up and get the underside, too). See page 52 for an easy baking soda–based hack to help freshen your sink.

Treat the trash.

A light weekly clean will stop smells from clinging to the can. Empty the can, and use a wet paper towel to wipe away any debris stuck inside or under the lid. Spray the whole thing, inside and out, with a disinfectant spray and let it dry.

LOAD the DISHWASHER PROPERLY

At the Institute, we've run thousands of cycles and found the best way to arrange things so every dish will come out sparkling.

Face dishes inward.
Load plates with the dirty sides facing the center, where the spray is the strongest.

Arrange utensils.
Forks: Prongs up

Spoons: Some up and some down to avoid nesting, which makes them harder to clean

Knives: Always with blades down for safety

Keep platters along the sides or back.
Placing these large dishes along the front of the bottom rack can prevent detergent from being fully dispensed and force you to run a second cycle to get everything clean.

Nestle glasses and mugs between tines.
You might think glasses should go over the tines, but that could lead to spots and cracks, if the glasses shift during the cycle.

Separate wineglasses.
Place them in the rack's stemware holders or nestle them securely between unbreakables. This will keep them from bumping into one another (or anything else) and possibly breaking.

Stop stacking.
While it's tempting to try to squeeze in as many dirty dishes as you can, this defeats the purpose: The water spray won't be able to reach (or clean) the dish that's on top.

Secure plastic items.
Blasts of water could cause lids or other small items to be dislodged and fall to the bottom. If there's an exposed heating element, they might melt.

SANITIZE CUTTING BOARDS

Plastic boards are easy to clean and can go into the dishwasher. Scrub wood boards in hot, sudsy water with a stiff dish brush, then dry. Condition wood cutting boards with a protective oil after cleaning. To help freshen and bleach out stains, go over any board with half a lemon dipped in salt. To sanitize boards: Mix 2 tsp. chlorine bleach and 1 gallon of water; carefully pour enough of the liquid on the board to cover it; let sit 2 minutes; air-dry; then wash and rinse the board. Keep separate boards for meats and vegetables to prevent contamination.

CARE for YOUR CLOTHES

Dust off that sewing machine, pull out that needle and thread, and try these DIY solutions for common clothing woes. Simple repairs can greatly extend the life of your clothing, offering ample reward for the time you put into upkeep.

How to Sew a Button

Don't toss the spare buttons that come with your clothes — save them in your sewing kit just in case.

1 Thread the needle. Double the string for more strength, and tie a knot at the end. Top your button with a toothpick to create extra slack so the button will be easier to use. Sew through the button's holes diagonally over the toothpick, back to front, forming an X, five to seven times, or until it feels secure.

2 As you end your last X, push the needle through the hole but not through the fabric. Remove the toothpick, taking care to maintain the slack you created.

3 Wrap the thread under and around the button about five times. This will keep the button in place on the thread and prevent it from ripping out of the fabric. Leave enough thread (1 to 2 inches) to tie the back knots.

4 Sew through the fabric beneath the button to the back of the fabric. Slide the needle through the back stitches to create a loop, then finish with a knot. Repeat until it feels secure. Snip off the remaining thread to finish.

> **LAB TIP** Hanging a buttoned shirt keeps it from getting wrinkled in your closet. Just make sure to button the shirt after you insert it into the hanger to avoid mangling the collar. If your collar gets wrinkled, a flat iron can give it a quick crisp-up.

How to Hem Anything

Shortening pants, skirts and dresses is much easier than you think.

1 Find your hem length.

Put on the item, and step into the shoes you'll wear with it most often. Stand up straight, look in a mirror and bend down to mark your preferred length all the way around with fabric chalk or sewing pins. (For best results, ask a friend for help.) Return to standing and make sure the hem falls evenly. Remove the garment. Don't worry if the hem now looks uneven.

2 Calculate seam allowance.

Use a tape measure to map out another line an inch below your initial hem marking. The space between the two lines is called the "seam allowance," and it's the fabric that's folded in to create a finished look and hide raw edges.

3 Trim away extra material.

Use fabric shears to trim carefully along the lower line. If you are hemming only a small amount of length, or if any of the original hem remains on the garment, remove it with a seam ripper to prevent chunkiness at the bottom.

4 Iron the new hem.

Turn the garment inside out and fold the edge of the fabric in so the first marked line serves as a clean bottom edge. Iron the fold for a crisp finish, and try on the garment again to be sure the length seems perfect. Use sewing pins to secure the fold.

5 Time to sew!

Turn the item inside out again, and stitch across the top of the fold. If sewing by hand, use stitches that are about a quarter of an inch apart. Turn the garment right side out, and you're done.

> **LAB TIP** No time to sew? Use hem fusible web tape. Cut a piece the length and width of the fallen hem. Sandwich it between the fabric layers and iron, following the package instructions.

GET RID of ANY STAIN

Regardless of the offender, follow these tips on washable fabrics for the best results.

Act fast.
The longer a stain sits, the harder it is to remove.

Blot, don't rub.
Rubbing only pushes a stain in deeper. Use a clean white cloth made of cotton (the most absorbent material), then begin at the stain's outer edges and work toward the center.

LAB TIP Save old towels; they do a great job of removing stains. You can also place the towel underneath the fabric to "pull" the stain out of the fabric while you treat it.

Be patient.
Don't rush the job. When dealing with stains, you need to give cleaning agents time to work their magic.

LAB TIP Unless you're sure a stain is gone, it's safest to air-dry a garment. Putting it through the dryer will set any residual stain, making it more difficult or even impossible to remove.

Test a hidden spot.
For safety, be sure to test any stain-removing method or product on a hidden spot of fabric. This is especially important with delicate upholstery. Always follow the label's recommended care instructions.

LAB TIP Assemble a stain-fighting kit, including white cloths for blotting, a spoon or dull knife for scraping, a carpet and upholstery cleaner, an eyedropper for a precise drop of bleach, a soft-bristled toothbrush for gently working stain remover into fabric and a spray bottle of cold water for rinsing.

Remove Common Stains

Stains happen—some more frequently than others.

Alcoholic Beverages

Sponge stain with cool water or soak item for about 30 minutes in cool water. Pretreat with a prewash stain remover. Launder. If it's safe for the fabric, add chlorine or all-fabric bleach.

LAB TIP The most common myth about how to remove red wine stains is the one about sprinkling salt on the stain — don't do it! Red wine stains contain tannin and can be set permanently by the application of salt.

Blood

If the stain is fresh, soak it in cold water or use an eye-dropper to apply hydrogen peroxide to it. For dried stains, brush it to remove the surface deposit, then soak in cool water with a laundry product containing enzymes. Launder in cold water with an enzyme detergent. If the stain remains, rewash with a fabric-safe bleach added.

Grass

Pretreat with a pre-wash stain remover, or rub liquid laundry detergent with enzymes into the stain. Launder using the hottest water safe for fabric plus chlorine or all-fabric bleach (if safe).

Ink

Sponge or soak the stain with rubbing alcohol. Rinse. If the stain remains, rub liquid laundry detergent into it and wash in the hottest water with a type of bleach that is safe for the fabric.

Sweat

If stain has changed the fabric's color, apply ammonia to fresh stains and white vinegar to old ones. Rinse. Pretreat with a prewash stain remover. Launder using the hottest water safe for the fabric. Stubborn stains may also respond to chlorine or oxygen bleach in the hottest water safe for the fabric.

SCAN ME!

HOW TO TACKLE MESSY CLOTHING STAINS

SIMPLIFY LAUNDRY DAY

Here's the easiest plan ever to follow.

Sort first, wash second.

Place a laundry hamper in each bedroom so family members can help keep clothing separated each time they undress. (This will also help prevent a clothes pileup on the floor.)

Choose the best setting.

One cycle doesn't fit all. You probably use the Regular or Delicate cycles most often, but other settings are worth exploring. They can offer extra rinses for bulky items or slower agitation for less wrinkling. Choose the shortest wash cycle to achieve good cleaning — no need to over-wash clothes.

Adjust load sizes.

Cramming the washtub with too many items isn't a useful shortcut — clothes need to move to get clean. Overloading your washer or dryer adds precious minutes (as the machine must work longer) and causes wrinkling while a too-small load means clothing may cling to the drum rather than tumble freely and easily. See pages 122–123 for fast fixes for common issues with washers and dryers.

Go easy on the dryer.

For bulky items, after your washing machine is finished, run a second spin cycle. This squeezes out excess water, so the dryer won't have to work as hard, shaving minutes off the process. If you have a newer high-efficiency machine, you can get the same results by selecting a higher spin-speed setting with your cycle.

Speed up (or skip) ironing.

For smooth results, remove garments from the dryer while they are still damp and iron immediately. If items are already dry, use the spray feature on your iron as you go to get wrinkles out faster.

Put it all away.

This final step can be just as daunting as washing, but getting your clothes and linens stored will make you feel incredibly productive. See pages 72–73 for tips on organizing your dresser drawers and conquering your closet.

SORT SMARTER

Start with color. Clothes with saturated colors and deep hues may be more likely to release dye, so group them together. If you have a possible bleeder (apply a drop of water and dab with a white paper towel to check), wash it separately the first few times.

Move on to fabric. Separate lint "givers" from lint "receivers." That means towels or fuzzy sweaters shouldn't be washed or dried with corduroy or velour. Also keep fabrics of similar weights together so coarse fabrics don't abrade and damage delicate ones.

Finish with soilage level. Very dirty or stained laundry needs extra attention in the form of more detergent or longer, more aggressive cycles. Sorting by the amount of soilage also keeps excess soil from redepositing on items that weren't that dirty in the first place.

Know When to Wash

If you're wondering whether it's time to do laundry, consult this handy chart.

AFTER EVERY WEAR

- ☐ Blouses/shirts
- ☐ Tights/socks
- ☐ Underwear

EVERY FEW WEARS/USES

- ☐ Bath towels
- ☐ Bras/camisoles
- ☐ Dresses/skirts
- ☐ Jeans/pants
- ☐ Pajamas
- ☐ Sweaters

EVERY 1 TO 2 DAYS

- ☐ Dishtowels
- ☐ Hand towels
- ☐ Washcloths

EVERY WEEK

- ☐ Bath mats
- ☐ Pillowcases
- ☐ Sheets

EVERY 1 TO 2 MONTHS

- ☐ Bathrobes
- ☐ Mattress pads
- ☐ Pillow liners

EVERY 3 TO 6 MONTHS

- ☐ Blankets and throws
- ☐ Comforters
- ☐ Decorative pillows
- ☐ Shower curtains
- ☐ Throw rugs

SCAN ME!

DECODE GARMENT LABELS

LAB TIP Prevent wrinkles by shaking items out before putting them into the dryer. Garments will tumble freely and dry more thoroughly. For minor wrinkles that have already set, use your fingers to sprinkle water on your garment, then gently tug to loosen the fibers and eliminate wrinkles. Hang to dry.

DECLUTTER in a WEEK

A quick task each day is all that's standing between you and the well-ordered home of your dreams. You'll be living clutter-free in just a week.

Day 1
Neaten your nightstand. Straighten things up and run a power strip across the back so you can charge your gadgets without cord chaos.

Day 2
Donate or recycle any duplicate flatware and kitchen tools, and invest in separators to keep drawers neat.

Day 3
Store bed linens neatly by putting a fitted sheet, one pillowcase and a matching duvet cover or flat sheet inside the other pillowcase. Grab the bundle when it's time to change the sheets. For how to fold a fitted sheet, see page 72.

Day 4
Put everything that doesn't belong in the kitchen or on the dining room table into a bin. Whichever member of the family has the most items in the bin must put everything away.

Day 5
Give half empties the heave-ho. Decant pasta, legumes, rice and cereal into airtight containers. Do the same in the bathroom, replacing crusty or ugly bottles with attractive ones for hand soap, shampoo and conditioner.

Day 6
Toss expired cleaning products in the bathroom and kitchen. See page 68 for information about safe disposal.

Day 7
Place similar items in the garage or shed in proximity (group together all sports gear, pet supplies, etc.).

EMBRACE THE "DROP ZONE"

It might seem counterintuitive to create a place where you leave piles of stuff. However, designating a single spot for everyday items is the stopgap that prevents your entire home from filling with unnecessary clutter.

ELIMINATE the REAL CAUSES of CLUTTER

Learn to let go of things. Imagine the worst-case scenario for getting rid of something. In most cases, you can probably borrow or repurchase the item if necessary.

Keep a donation bag or box

in your closet or near the front door to make donating easier. You'll feel good knowing your clothes or stuff will find a new home.

Get help with tasks.

Assign clear responsibilities, communicate them and give consequences when they're not accomplished.

Stop procrastinating.

Don't delay decisions about where to put things — or wait to put them there. Resist the urge to "just put it here for now."

Give everything a home.

If you can't find a place for the item, perhaps it's not right for you or your home.

LAB TIP Answering a few questions will help you determine what to bring into your home.

1. Who owns it already and might share it with me?

2. What do I have at home that is similar?

3. Where will it be stored?

4. When will I have time to use and maintain it?

5. Why do I really want to buy it?

SAY "THANKS, BUT NO THANKS"

If you aren't going to use something someone wants to give you, it's OK to say no. Try one of these responses:

"Thank you, but I don't have very much storage space right now."

"Thank you, but those seasons and sizes aren't going to match up with our kids."

"Thank you, but these won't work for our lifestyle. You probably have another friend who could use them."

DISPOSE of EVERYTHING SAFELY

Disposal can get a little tricky when it comes to items such as appliances, electronics and old medications. When in doubt, contact your local sanitation department.

Batteries
Recycle
Rechargeable batteries (such as the ones in cell phones and other electronics) may contain hazardous chemicals. Check with your local sanitation department to find recycling locations.

Avoid throwing single-use batteries into the trash.

Books
Donate or recycle
Donate gently used books to local libraries, schools or thrift stores.

Paperbacks can be recycled, but remove the cover binding before recycling hardcovers.

Cell Phone
Donate or recycle
Before getting rid of your old cell phone, delete your personal information using a factory or hard reset option (check the manufacturer's website for details).

Cleaning Products
Trash or recycle
Check the bottle's label for information about proper disposal. Rinse the bottle before recycling.

Clothes
Donate
Donate gently used clothes.

Coffee Pods
Recycle or reuse
Check with the manufacturer, which might offer recycling options. Alternatively, you can use them to freeze herbs, grow seedlings or store office supplies like paper clips.

Electronics
Recycle
Check with the manufacturer to see about trade-in or recycling options.

Eyeglasses

Donate

Ask your optometrist for recommendations about where to donate your old specs.

Kitchenware

Donate or recycle

Donate pots and pans to thrift stores, or recycle kitchenware through your local sanitation department.

Light Bulbs

Recycle or trash

Some states and jurisdictions may require that light bulbs be recycled, so check your local laws before tossing these in the trash.

Mattress

Trash or donate

Some cities will collect your mattress if you put it out with regular garbage for bulk collection. Many retailers haul the old one away for you when you buy a new one.

Medication

Trash

Dispose of expired or unused medication as soon as possible to prevent others from accidentally taking or intentionally misusing them.

Call your local pharmacy with questions.

Microwave and Small Appliances

Donate, trash or recycle

Donate usable appliances. Some municipalities let you recycle broken microwaves, blenders and toasters as scrap metal. Check with your local sanitation department. Otherwise, throw out broken items.

Refrigerator and Freezer

Trash

Contact your local sanitation department to schedule removal, or check the Environmental Protection Agency's Responsible Appliance Disposal website to find a partner program near you.

Washer and Dryer

Donate or recycle

If they're still in good working order, donate them.

You can also check with your local sanitation department for proper disposal.

OVERCOME SECRET SOURCES of CHAOS

Even the most organized among us has a drawer or area that seems utterly resistant to taming.

	On Top of Your Desk	In the Junk Drawer	In the Bathroom	On Top of Your Dresser
THE PROBLEM	**Unsorted stacks can lead to past-due bills, over-looked offers and more.**	**Turn this black hole into a place where necessary supplies are found, not lost.**	**How many barely used lipsticks and sunscreens have you had to throw away?**	**Your dresser doesn't need to be a dumping ground.**
THE EASY FIX	Practice the "ART" of managing paper as soon as a piece enters your home: "Action" items, like bills, should be placed in a tray and addressed once a week; "Reference" items go right into your filing system; and "Trash" should be recycled or shredded immediately.	An insert with customizable compartments is the fastest way to organize this drawer. Slide coupons, pens, rubber bands and other sundry items into their own sections. Then tuck less frequently used items like twist ties in labeled mint tins.	Limit your stock of beauty supplies. Have one zippered pouch for nail polish, one shelf for skin care and one bin for haircare. When the space is full, don't add a thing until you get rid of something. Keep daily products in sight and occasional items under the sink.	If you apply makeup in your bedroom, place items in a tray, box or bag to keep them from migrating along the dresser top. A small decorative tray keeps perfumes organized and protects your dresser from drips or spills.
HABITS THAT STICK	Start thinking of your desk as a kitchen sink. You likely have a rule for how long you allow dirty dishes to sit — apply the same mentality to avoid late-fee charges on your bills, or eliminate paper bills entirely by automating bill-paying.	Before you stash it, ask yourself, Is there a better home for this? Batteries should go in the utility room, stamps in the desk and bandages in the bathroom.	Use a permanent marker to label bottles, tubes and jars with their purchase dates so you can better track your spending and see when an item is past its prime.	Every dresser needs a holder for small items like change, keys and rings. It can be a simple cup, bowl or basket, or something more decorative, like a tiered serving dish or tray.

Make Your Own Cubbies

Wrangle clutter with an inexpensive storage unit that can be tailored to fit any space. Even better, this project doesn't require a single power tool to construct.

1 Decorate the crates.
Purchase plain wooden crates at the craft store, then paint the inside of the box or leave it bare and simple.

2 Clip them together.
Stack and restack them until you find the right configuration. Try a pyramid, or a low horizontal design behind a sofa or beneath a TV. Found your arrangement? Fasten the sides of the adjoining crates with large binder clips (measure the crate thickness first to ensure a snug fit). Avoid stashing heavy things like appliances near the top so the crates won't topple.

CONQUER YOUR CLOSETS

Never fear opening the door again.

Linen Closet

Drape blankets on the door.
Install a couple of slim towel bars to keep throws handy yet tidy.

Add a tray for table linens.
You'll be able to carry everything to the table to set it.

Tuck bedding in baskets. Give sheet sets a labeled drop spot, and you won't have to stress about folding that fitted sheet perfectly anymore. Or slide a set of sheets into a matching pillowcase (see page 66).

Make more room for towels.
Use hanging shelves for hand towels so they don't get swallowed by stacks.

Clothing Closet

Keep accessories handy. Try a door-mounted organizer for scarves, hats and more. With these outfit makers grouped together, getting dressed is a snap.

Prevent piles. Stacks of anything tend to fall over. Easy-to-install dividers (they slip onto the existing shelf) keep everything in place without the need for closed bins.

Streamline your hangers. Thin, velvety styles grip clothes, but they don't take up as much room as wood or plastic hangers.

FOLD A FITTED SHEET

1. Hold the sheet. Place your hands in the corners with the long side of the sheet going across your body and the top of the fabric facing you.

2. Tuck the corners. Take one corner in your hand, and tuck it into the other. Repeat the tuck on the opposite side. Now your sheet is folded in half.

3. Repeat the tuck. With your hands in the corners again, repeat the tuck one more time so that all four corners are now folded into each other.

4. Lay the sheet down. Place the sheet on a flat surface like a table, countertop or bed. You should see a C shape in the fabric.

5. Fold in thirds. Fold the edges from the outside in, smoothing as you go. Fold in thirds again from the other direction. Flip it over, and you're done!

ORDER YOUR DRESSER DRAWERS

Here's how to get yours into excellent shape.

Invest in dividers.

Spring-loaded flexible inserts transform a cluttered underwear drawer into a streamlined system that's as beautiful as it is functional. Start by editing out tattered, ill-fitting or uncomfortable items. Group undies by type (brief, bikini, etc.). For bras, fold one cup into the other so they keep their shape and take up less space. If you have the room, skip folding and instead layer them in a stack with one tucked behind the other.

File your T-shirts.

Apply this office strategy to your clothes drawer: Instead of piling T-shirts on top of one another in drawers, fold them a bit smaller and "file" them from front to back with the folded edges facing up. You'll find what you need immediately, and when you pull one out, the others will remain neatly in place. Color-code from light to dark for added organization.

Roll with it.

Slippery garments like pajamas, silk lingerie, scarves and camisoles get messy when folded and stacked in a drawer. Instead, roll them and line them up in a row. Tuck pajama tops into bottoms and roll them together. Line all the rolls up cleanly so you can more easily find and remove just what you're looking for.

Fold pants properly.

This super-condensed way of folding allows you to pack more pants into each drawer: Fold the pants in half, placing one leg on top of the other with the back pockets facing out. Fold in half lengthwise, bringing the hem to just below the waist and forming a long rectangle. Fold the pants upward again, this time into thirds.

Consider hanging sweaters.

If you've run out of space to stack them, you can hang sweaters instead. But don't hang a sweater as you would a blouse. Instead, fold it in half vertically, matching up the sleeves, then place the hook of the hanger at the armpit. Fold the sleeves over one side of the hanger and the body over the other. This keeps the sweater from stretching and prevents those annoying little shoulder bumps.

CORRAL KID STUFF

One of the biggest challenges of parenthood is conquering your children's toys. Our advice: Lean into kids' natural tendencies to sort, organize and play games.

Make it fun.
Turn cleanup into a game by singing a funny song or challenging your kids to see who can clean up the fastest.

Model good habits.
So much of parenting is about saying the same thing over and over, but it's also about making sure that you practice what you preach and show how to take care of your stuff.

Teach the "one in, one out" rule.
Kids need to understand that storage is finite, and that continuing to collect eventually leads to clutter and chaos. When they get a new toy or new jeans, send an old item to the donation bin.

Color-code.
Give everyone a color, then use that color throughout your home — think hampers, backpacks, toothbrushes and towels — to keep everyone organized and make cleanup a snap.

Think small, lidless bins.
Use them on a low shelf to make them as accessible as possible, and store anything and everything in them.

LAB TIP Oily hands and snack stains making playing cards grimy and putting a damper on game night? Try this shake-and-clean trick: Place the cards in a paper bag along with a few tablespoons of cornstarch or flour. Give them a shake, and then wipe clean with a paper towel.

DO a DIGITAL RESET

Your devices should make your life easier, not harder. Here's how to avoid clutter and keep them working their best.

Establish email blocks.

Schedule time to tackle your inbox so it doesn't derail your day. Dive in no more than once an hour and no less than once a day, depending on urgency.

Corral cords.

Electrical cords are dust magnets. Avoid this by zip-tying them together or tacking them up off the floor.

Reduce glare.

Harsh light reflection can make it hard to see and cause eyestrain. To reduce glare at a computer, adjust the angle and height of your screen as well as your sitting position. It also helps to clean the screen, place an anti-glare cover on it and increase the brightness.

Keep gadgets dust-free.

Stow microfiber cloths and screen-cleaning spray in a drawer, basket or bin near your charging station so you can spruce up items as you take them out. Stash an extra microfiber cloth in your device's carrying case (or a purse pocket) for on-the-go cleaning.

Resist the upgrade.

Instead, extend the life of the device you already have by getting it repaired.

Donate or recycle the clunkers.

Old electronics can leak mercury and lead into the soil. See page 68 for more advice about safely disposing of gadgets and other goods. Don't forget your cords as well.

LAB TIP Experts recommend deep cleaning your phone at least twice a week to remove any bacteria or viruses. Here's how:

1. Remove your phone from its case, and power it down.

2. Polish with a microfiber cloth.

3. Use a disinfecting wipe.

4. Air-dry for up to 5 minutes.

5. Wipe it down once more with a clean paper towel or microfiber cloth.

6. Repeat steps 2–5 with your phone case.

LAB TIP There are lots of upgrades you can make to your home, but a new paint color might have the biggest impact on any room. Or better yet, go with two colors! Layering a light and dark color will give the room automatic depth, and it's easy to do with a neutral like ivory and a complex color like navy blue.

CHAPTER 3

DECORATE & RENOVATE

TRY a MINI-MAKEOVER for MAXIMUM IMPACT

It doesn't take much to make over your space. In fact, a few tweaks can help any room in your home go from drab to fab.

Choose a color palette.
Pick three colors, then keep your decor in that family. Select colors that match one another or speak to you.

Embrace negative space.
Always allow breathing room, particularly in places that have feature walls or dramatic accents.

Hang some art or photos.
Nothing cheers up a room quite like photos of your favorite smiling faces or an affordable piece that moves you. An oversize print can turn a boring wall into a decorative highlight. On page 85, learn how to create a gallery wall.

Play with textiles.
Drape a throw wherever you could use a little coziness. Place a super-soft one on the back of a stiff chair, or hang a colorful quilt to add personality to a blank wall (for more tips on conquering a blank wall, see page 97).

Create conversation zones.
Reposition furniture to encourage family members and guests to chat and enjoy each other's company. Simply put, chairs should face each other — not the TV.

Mix patterns.
Use a few of your favorite prints for pieces like seating and window treatments, but stick to the same color family for a cohesive look.

Start small.
Add an area rug, change out the lampshades, replace your duvet or hand towels. A new piece might be all the change you need to fall back in love with your space.

Choose task-related lights.
Pick lamps or fixtures according to the activities that will take place in each zone. A floor lamp with a bold bulb makes reading easy, while a soft glow is best for evening lounging.

BRIGHTEN YOUR KITCHEN

Bring happy to your kitchen with fun patterns and bold colors.

Paint the floors.
Transform hardwood floors with painter's tape, glossy paint and a weekend's work. Use a solid color, try a "mock tile" look with diamonds, or even add stripes for a show-stopping display.

Switch out cabinet hardware.
If you're not ready to invest in new cabinetry, a drawer-pull swap can give your kitchen a quick upgrade. Go for a modern, sleek feel with a bar pull, or add some personality with a colorful ceramic knob.

Display your favorite plates.
Keep heirlooms, thrift store finds and sunny serveware where everyone can enjoy them. For extra flair, consider installing removable wallpaper to really make the backs of your shelves pop.

Add a colorful appliance.
Make cooking fun with statement kitchen gadgets. Start small with a bright blender or go all out with a pastel oven.

CALM YOUR BEDROOM

Turn your bedroom into the ultimate relaxation zone.

Keep surfaces clear.

Hang clothes in the closet instead of piling them on a chair, and limit items on your bedside table to a few things you need, like a lamp, a ring dish and a basket to store bedtime reading. Avoid leaving unfinished work or your laptop lying around: Your bedroom should be a place to unwind.

Add sentimental pieces.

A tidy space doesn't have to be sterile. Put what gives you peace within eyesight, whether that's a favorite snapshot or a trinket passed down for generations.

Pick soft textures in muted colors.

A tufted headboard, velvety pillows and a luxurious knitted throw add coziness that will have you wanting to linger in bed every morning. Neutral colors are easy on the eye, and the mix of materials creates visual interest.

BEAUTIFY YOUR BATHROOM

Thoughtful organization and beautiful accents create a bathroom oasis.

Add a plant (or two).

Try a small potted orchid, or place a no-nonsense asparagus fern in a corner; either will thrive in humidity. For more info on picking your perfect plant, see page 104.

Match your storage.

Baskets in the same neutral shades will look uniform even if their shapes and sizes are differ-ent. Keep linens neatly folded, and corral toiletries into catchalls.

Change out hand towels.

And your bath mat while you're at it. This inexpensive upgrade instantly revives a tired bathroom.

COZY UP YOUR LIVING ROOM

Impress guests with a living room that invites conversation.

SCAN ME!
FURNITURE MAKING 101: BEGINNER'S FARMHOUSE TABLE (UNDER $100)!

Offer plenty of seating.

A comfy couch is important, but accent chairs or an oversize ottoman will give everyone a place to relax. Pressed for space? Keep a couple of fluffy floor pillows in a closet to bring out when you have unexpected guests.

Use tricks to make the most of every inch.

A rounded coffee table literally cuts corners and opens up your space. Layering rugs helps define the sitting area, and high-hanging curtains draw the eye upward.

Add lived-in touches.

Rooms that look as if people live in them make friends and family feel right at home. Instead of fussy accents no one is allowed to touch, decorate with stacks of well-loved books and beloved mementoes.

Choose statement lighting.

Give guests something to talk about with a bright chandelier. The extra light will open up the room, while the design serves as a conversation starter.

CREATE a GALLERY WALL

A gallery wall is a great way to display some of your favorite photos, art and souvenirs. When hanging, think personality over perfection. The best part of a gallery wall is that it doesn't have to be perfect.

1 Match frames.

To create a collage that looks luxe, hang a cluster of frames that are the same size and made of the same material. Alternatively, you can use a variety of frame shapes and sizes, hanging some vertically and others horizontally, for an intriguing display.

2 Go beyond photos and art.

Frame personal keepsakes like ticket stubs, flea market finds or woven baskets. Group images by subject — say, landscapes or dogs — to tie together an arrangement.

3 Plan your placement.

Avoid errant nail holes by putting frames on the ground in front of the wall to try different arrangements and spacing, or trace the frames on craft paper and tape cutouts to the wall; adjust till you love the look. Experiment with different layouts to see what works best.

4 Measure your laid-out frames and the wall area.

Generally, leave 2 inches between outer edges of frames (maybe less only when they're the same size or shape). Keep distance between frames as consistent as possible.

5 Hang from the middle out.

Start by hanging the picture that will go in the middle of the arrangement, then work your way out. Once there's a basic framework on the wall, you can always add to it later.

SCAN ME!

HOW TO MAKE AN EASY DIY GALLERY WALL WITH WILL TAYLOR

FIND A STUD IN A WALL

1. Look for a light switch or a power outlet, as electrical boxes are often attached to studs. Pinpoint the one nearest to the area where you want to place something that requires extra reinforcement, like heavy artwork or a large TV.

2. Measure 16 inches from the switch, which is the typical distance between studs. Keep in mind that some are placed 24 inches apart, so you may have to measure a second time.

3. Knock or tap the wall gently with your fist or a hammer wrapped in a dishtowel. If you hear a hollow or empty sound, tap a little to the left and right. When the sound is muffled, you've hit the stud!

4. Confirm by drilling a hole. You'll know you've hit wood if you feel pressure against the drill bit. If you can't find the stud even after drilling, fish around behind the wall with a wire hanger until you hit it.

ENLARGE a SMALL SPACE

Use ingenuity and imagination to make the best of a tiny room.

Think in sections.

Divide a room geometrically into quarters, thirds or halves, then assign each section a function — like sleeping or eating — and design around that function.

Pick lighter colors for walls and floors.

Lighter tones give the illusion of more space.

Choose furniture that does double duty.

A daybed tucked into a reading nook works equally well for lazy Sundays and houseguests.

Go full size.

Select a few full-size furniture pieces instead of cramming in lots of smaller ones. The room will feel more expansive.

Fake a window with an oversize mirror.

It acts like another window and creates a bright focal point.

Leave some openness.

Resist the urge to cram a small space with tons of stuff.

Set things back.

Recessed shelving gives depth to tight quarters.

A wall-mounted shelf can double as a narrow desk.

Don't overlook the space under the stairs.

LAB TIP Here's how to determine the ideal height for hanging anything: eye level is 57 to 60 inches from the floor. Since the middle of the painting should sit at this height, you'll need to do some math to get it just right. Take the height of the frame, divide it by 2, subtract the distance from the top of the frame to the hardware, then add 60.

WOW with WALLPAPER

Wallpaper is the best way to infuse personality and pattern into your space. There are options for nearly every room and aesthetic, from rainbow-inspired florals to neutral geometrics to simple stripes.

1 **Try removable wallpaper** for a low-key commitment. (No glue required!) To ensure you line up the pattern properly, start from the top and smooth with a roller.

2 **Use texture to create depth.** Wallpaper made of tweed, grasscloth and bamboo will do exactly that.

3 **Make your own wallpaper** by layering dozens of magazine, newspaper or book pages to craft a custom wall covering using peel-and-stick adhesive.

4 **Get creative with wallpaper scraps.** Rather than tossing oddly shaped pieces of wallpaper, try a delightfully unexpected decorating hack like wallpapering the riser of your stairs or the inside of your coat closet, or framing swatches for elegant (and easy) art.

LAB TIP To zap bubbles, use a roller for removable wallpaper. Pop stubborn ones with a pin, then smooth. For nonremovable wallpaper, fill a syringe with a bit of wallpaper paste, then squirt directly into the bubble and smooth. For bigger bubbles, make an X over the bubble with a utility knife, then carefully apply paste to each flap using a syringe or brush. Tamp the flaps down. Be careful about using too much paste, as that can cause bubbling elsewhere. Wipe off any excess paste with a damp cloth.

WHERE TO WALLPAPER

Here are a few natural locations for a bit of flair:

Hallways
Although you might be reluctant to install graphic wallpaper in your living room or bedroom, it's perfect for a hallway. Stay on theme by opting for a rug and light fixture in the same hues as your wallpaper.

Small Spaces
Papering the walls from floor to ceiling gives even the tiniest of rooms extra height. Keep the flow going.

Ceilings (a.k.a. the "Fifth Wall")
Often forgotten, ceilings are a blank canvas for florals, stripes and other simple patterns. Paint the walls in a complementary shade.

Inside Shelving
Upgrade basic built-ins or a standard bookcase into a focal point. Remove the shelves (if you can) to cover the back in one fell swoop. Otherwise, cut peel-and-stick wallpaper to the correct size for each cubby.

PAINT a ROOM in a DAY

Achieve professional results in just seven steps.

1 Make a plan.

Before you ever pick up a paintbrush, you need a plan of attack. Does the ceiling need a refresh, too? What about the trim? Consider your options on the walls as well. Will you be using one color — or do you want to try painting with two colors (an accent wall, perhaps)?

2 Gather the proper materials.

The surface and size of what you're painting will determine the exact supplies you need, but it's a good idea to stock your tool kit with the following:

- Painter's tape
- Drop cloths
- Paint roller
- Paintbrushes (both angled and straight)
- Paint tray
- Stir stick
- Paint

Other worthy investments: An extension pole, so you can stash away the ladder after edging; a paint-can opener and a pour spout to lessen mess.

3 Prep the room for painting.

Paint won't adhere to a dirty surface, so dust the walls floor to ceiling and scrub any grime with a wet sponge or cloth. Let dry before you paint.

Protect the floor and any furniture you can't move from paint splatters and spills. Lay fabric drop cloths on the floor, as plastic can become slick underfoot or beneath the ladder.

Remove outlet and light switch plates and tape around any areas you don't want painted (such as moldings, baseboards or window frames) with painter's masking tape.

4 Prime the wall (or don't with our handy trick).

Painting over a dark wall with a light color (or covering stains) requires a coat of primer and two coats of paint — and at least 6 hours of drying time. Painting a humid room or on a humid day will take longer. You can also opt for self-priming paint. Going from light to light? You can get away with skipping primer and using two coats of good-quality regular paint.

(continued on page 92)

5 Mix the paint.

Though the store generally shakes the paint for you, a decent stir will ensure your paint is properly mixed. This is particularly important if the can has been sitting on a shelf for any length of time. Though an optional step, you can also strain the paint to get rid of any impurities.

LAB TIP **Have a moist rag handy to wipe fresh splatters. Scrape off dried drips with a credit card or plastic spatula.**

6 Get rolling.

With an angled brush, or a sponge tool to "cut in," paint a 2-inch swath around the edges of woodwork and the ceiling. Use a roller cover with a $\frac{1}{4}$-inch nap for smooth surfaces, $\frac{3}{8}$-inch nap for semi-smooth or $\frac{5}{8}$-inch nap for rough — the wrong tool will apply too much or too little paint. If using a latex paint, pre-wet the roller and then wring out most of the water.

Fill the well of the paint tray about a quarter of the way. Then, when loading the paint, roll the roller back and forth in the well until it is uniformly covered. Finally, move the roller back and forth in the upper portion to remove any excess.

Fill in the central unpainted space using the roller. Paint the wall in overlapping W- or M-shaped strokes for the most even paint distribution. Let the first coat dry at least a couple of hours, then coat again. Between coats, cover the tray and brush with plastic wrap touching the paint surface (to prevent the paint from drying out), and refrigerate.

LAB TIP **If you're painting a room with two colors — stripes, for example — start with the lighter color first. Once it's dry, run painter's tape over the divider, then paint the darker color.**

7 Finish and clean up.

Rinse your paintbrush and roller under a faucet until the water runs clear. Decant the tray's leftover paint back into the can; seal the can tightly by placing a paper towel over the lid and tapping the lid edges with a hammer. Rinse the tray.

Once the brush's bristles are totally dry, slip the brush back into its original paper wrapper to keep the bristles from fanning out, or try this DIY fix: Fold a thick piece of paper around the bristles; tape to secure.

PICK the PERFECT PAINT COLOR

Start by thinking about what you ultimately want. Do you envision a warm or a cool shade? Does your space warrant a bold color, or would a neutral be more appropriate? Once you have a general idea of the direction you want to go in, you can begin sifting through paint chips and pick a few finalists.

Paint a sample swatch.

Colors often look brighter once on the wall, and the light in your room can have a dramatic impact on the way the color reads. To give you a good idea of how the color will look in your space, paint two coats of color in a 12-by-12-inch square. If your room has both sunny and shady spots, it's smart to put swatches in both areas, as the amount of natural light can affect the final look.

Test multiple colors with foam board.

Alternatively, you can paint two coats onto a foam board (available at any craft or office supply store) and tape it to the wall. This is a great option for those who don't intend to get started right away, since you won't have to live with random color streaks on your walls.

LAB TIP Use a foam brush for this type of sample painting. You won't dirty a ton of brushes or waste money.

Calculate how much paint you need.

Many retailers have helpful calculators you can use. Always double-check packaging, but in general, a gallon is roughly good for 250 to 400 square feet. And don't forget: You'll need a little extra for touch-ups and mistakes.

LAB TIP White can be either warm or cool, depending on the shade. Whites with pink undertones will appear warmer than whites with gray or blue undertones. If you're still not sure whether a particular shade is warm or cool, hold the swatch or item in question next to a pure version of that color (such as a true white from the color wheel). You'll quickly determine which way it leans.

CHOOSE an ACCENT WALL

An accent wall is a great option for any room that lacks visual interest — it infuses a space with character without being overwhelming.

Wallpaper it.
Pick a pattern that shows off a piece of furniture, or let a pretty pattern function like an oversize painting. For more details about wowing with wallpaper, see page 89.

Cork it.
If you like the look of collages and need ample space to keep your to-do list on full display in your home office, deck out a wall in cork square panels. It's the perfect blend of style and function.

Mirror it.
A group of mirrors can help a cozy space feel much brighter. Hang your favorites to allow light to bounce around the space.

Color it.
A room full of brilliant walls could be intense, but a single wall of emerald green, royal blue or equally rich color creates a warm and inviting atmosphere.

Map it.
Colorful maps double as artwork — and create a world-traveler vibe in any space. Simply overlap the maps and tack them onto the wall.

Divide it.
A two-tone wall draws the eye upward. Go with a darker color on the bottom half of the wall and save a hue a few shades lighter for the top portion.

Collage it.
Scour thrift shops for a motley collection of shutters, and then paint them in soothing blues and greens.

Clad it.
Cover a wall in horizontal planks known as shiplap for a dose of farmhouse charm and instant texture. Shiplap also offers the illusion of space.

LAB TIP To pick the best spot for an accent wall, pinpoint where your eyes land when you first enter the room.

SCAN ME!
HOW TO PAINT MODERN WALL STENCILING WITH ED ROTH

ARRANGE a BOOKSHELF

The styling opportunities for bookshelves are endless. You can decorate shelves with artwork or lush greenery, dress them up with a trendy paint color or wallpaper, and stack books vertically or horizontally. Add a comfortable chair and soft lighting to make your reading experience as enjoyable as possible.

Organize reads (and other items) by color.
Your heart will see everything you love, but your head will be satisfied by the order. Keep dust jackets on, or remove them for a cleaner look.

Think scale.
Every bookshelf deserves that one oversize statement piece, like a brass geometric sculpture or a heartwarming black-and-white photograph.

Add color.
Paint or paper the back of your bookcases to make your favorite titles pop.

Intersperse meaningful mementoes.
If you love them, they'll always look great together. Balance the display with color-coordinated books.

Keep the shelves airy.
Avoid overfilling your shelf to maintain a sense of lightness and space.

Include framed photos.
Display coordinating frames both in and on your bookcase. This quirky move adds an element of surprise design, but also creates a room that feels lived in.

Corral clutter.
A row of similar baskets acts as a visual anchor and makes it easy to stow displaced objects. For more tips on conquering clutter, see page 66.

Go high.
If you have a collection — vintage fans, for instance — make them a part of your bookshelf setup. Fill the empty space on top of your shelves with your treasured finds.

Scatter in succulents.
Adding plants is a great way to clear the air and bring the outdoors in. See page 104 for more info.

LAB TIP **Follow the rule of three. Open shelves are great in theory — until you fill them with knickknacks, collections and straight-up clutter. Aim for no more than three nonbook items per shelf, and use color or theme to unite the pieces, such as three silver frames.**

REFINISH FURNITURE — with PAINT

Take everyday items from tired to terrific with just a fresh coat of paint.

1

2

3

4

1 Prep

Remove hardware and take out any drawers. Clean dirt from surface by sponging with soap and water; let dry.

2 Sand

Sand in a circular motion with medium-grit paper to remove any existing paint or stain and smooth out the surface. (Do this over a floor covered with newsprint.) Sweep off dust and wipe with a clean, damp cloth.

3 Prime

Primer blocks old color and creates a new surface for your paint to stick to. Check the paint you'll be using for its primer recommendations. Use painter's tape to protect any areas you don't want to paint. In a well-ventilated spot — a covered outdoor area is best — lay a canvas drop cloth on the floor, then apply primer, giving it plenty of time to dry, anywhere from 30 minutes to 4 hours.

4 Paint & Finish

Apply paint in thin layers and give each one time to dry completely. You'll need to apply at least two coats of paint — more for warm colors like reds and oranges. Wait at least 72 hours for the paint to cure before replacing drawers, attaching knobs or placing anything on the surface of your piece.

LAB TIP Add peel-and-stick patterned wallpaper inside drawers for extra flare. Cut sheets to fit with a craft knife, remove the backing and work from one corner to another, pressing out air bubbles as you go.

Bright color breathes new life into an old piece of furniture.

PAINT CHEAT SHEET

These chic paint styles will transform your furniture:

Antiqued Metal
Use a 1- to 2-inch nylon/polyester brush to apply this syrupy paint in very thin coats. Let dry completely (about 24 hours) between coats.

Whitewashed
Make sure any trace of preexisting stain is removed first. Use a natural-bristle brush to coat a small section with this thin formula, then use a rag to wipe it, in the direction of the grain, before starting the next section.

Flea Market Chic
Using a natural-bristle brush, apply two coats of a lighter shade, then one of a darker shade; let dry for at least 24 hours. Wearing a mask, rub gently with medium-grit sandpaper until the bottom coat starts to show.

LAB TIP Instead of reupholstering furniture, try painting it to save the curves, tufts and trim of a chair you love. This process is typically better for accent pieces than, say, your family couch, as it will leave your furniture a bit stiffer than it was before. Use one part latex satin paint, one part fabric medium and two parts water. Let each coat dry completely.

DISCOVER NEW USES for OLD THINGS

Just about anything can be completely transformed into a one-of-a-kind item and conversation starter.

Window Frame
Sand away blemishes on an old window frame, then use painter's tape to give a fresh coat of color. Paint one pane with chalkboard paint, and cover another with adhesive-backed cork roll. Then add a shelf and hooks, and you've got a cute organizer for the entryway.

Cabinet Cheese Board
With paint and a pair of drawer pulls, a salvaged cabinet door becomes a makeshift cheese board or TV dinner tray. To make, fill holes in the board with wood filler and let dry. Sand and paint the surface, predrill holes and screw in handles.

Pom-Pom Trim
Put a pom-pom on it! Existing curtains, throw pillows or lampshades (like those at right) get a fun makeover with pom-pom or fringe trim. Pick a trim color that pops against the other shades in your space for maximum impact.

Wool Coasters
Salvage a shrunken sweater by turning it into coasters. Wash 100% wool in hot water, then dry with an agitator like jeans. After three rounds, the sweater should feel taut and felt-like. Use a large-mouthed glass to trace circles onto the fabric and then snip out a set.

Dresser Kitchen Island
Turn an old dresser into a kitchen island with lots of storage by covering the back with chalkboard paint.

Shoe Holder
Hang an over-the-door shoe holder on a fence, tucking herbs into the compartments for a quick vertical planter.

Brass Thumbtack Accents
Push or tap brass tacks along the lines of a table, bench or chair for added sparkle and shine.

Headboard Ladder
Turned on its side, a slatted headboard becomes an eye-catching space to display blankets and throws.

FIND YOUR PERFECT PLANT

Use our handy chart of hardy indoor species to find your botanical soulmate.

CHALLENGE	SUGGESTED PLANT	WHY IT'S PERFECT
There's an awkward spot	Snake plant	**The vertical swordlike** foliage of a snake plant makes an eye-catching addition to any room. Also called *Sansevieria*, this popular plant takes low light and little water while growing fast and tall.
You have a brown thumb	ZZ plant	**Virtually indestructible,** *Zamioculcas zamiifolia* — better known as the ZZ plant — seems to thrive in harsh conditions and neglect, including low light and lack of watering. It's ideal for beginners, or people convinced they have a brown thumb.
You want to fill a dark corner	Heartleaf philodendron	**There's a lot to love** about philodendrons, including their heart-shaped leaves. This low-maintenance plant tolerates low light and should dry out slightly between waterings.
You have a large, open corner	Dragon tree	**With dramatic foliage** and detailed markings, this popular houseplant is a great way to fill up free space. Over time, *Dracaena* will reach a height of 3 feet, so make sure it has plenty of room to grow, along with moderate light and slightly moist soil.
The room is bathed in flourescent light	Golden pothos	**This hardy vining plant** has glossy variegated leaves that drape perfectly over dressers, shelves or hanging planters, even in fluorescent light. Use hooks to help pothos frame a window or bookshelf. It also goes by the name "devil's ivy" because it's very hard to kill.

CHALLENGE	SUGGESTED PLANT	WHY IT'S PERFECT
You sometimes forget you have plants	Succulents	**These waxy,** geometric plants have thick leaves that store water, so they typically only require weekly watering (wait until the soil is dry before dousing them again). All succulents generally enjoy sunlight and dry air.
You're a frequent traveler	Fiddle-leaf fig tree	**This beauty** can survive for two weeks without water. Young plants feature dense foliage, but that spreads out as they age and grow more "treelike." Give your fiddle-leaf fig tree bright, indirect light — an east-facing window is perfect. Water once the top inch of soil is dry, drench until water comes out the bottom of the pot and then let it dry out again.
The space is very humid	Maidenhair fern	**The delicate,** lacy fronds of maidenhair fern absolutely adore high humidity. Give this plant bright, indirect light (no direct sun or it will burn), and constant, light moisture, as in a sunny bathroom.
The room gets intense, direct sunlight	Cacti	**Bunny-eared** *Opuntia* cacti produce prickly pads, while barrel cacti with their bright yellow spines are perfect for growing on windowsills. They will withstand most maltreatment except for heavy-handed watering and feeding.
The room gets low, indirect light	Bird's-nest fern	**Fern plants** are the be-all and end-all of houseplants. They've been around for millions of years, thriving in all kinds of light and water conditions. Bird's-nest fern enjoys low light.
You have curious pets	Rattlesnake plant	**Many houseplants** are toxic to pets, but not this one. The *Calathea* plant's reptilelike, two-tone leaves will add interest to any tabletop — and the plant loves low light.
There is zero counter space	Spider plant	**Spider plants** have long strappy leaves and arching stems with tiny plantlets on the ends, which can be pinched off to make new baby plants. Hang yours in a room with bright light. Water it when the soil is slightly dry.

CHARM YOUR HOUSEPLANTS

Once you've picked your perfect plants, use these tips to help them thrive. And see page 151 for everything you need to know to grow a container garden.

Water wisely.
Some plants love to sit in oodles of water; others require just a taste.

Add a filter.
Before you fill your pot with soil, line the bottom with a coffee filter. This will allow excess water to flow through the drainage hole while keeping dirt where it belongs.

Mix in some coffee grounds.
When blended with your potting soil, ground coffee, rich in nutrients, can help your plants grow. It's a smart addition to your compost pile too. For more info on composting, see page 161.

Start with citrus.
Save juiced lemon halves for sprouting seedlings. After the seed germinates, you can plant the whole thing (lemon rind and all) in a pot or the garden.

Sneak in a sponge.
Placing a sponge at the bottom of the pot will collect excess water that your plant can continue to drink if you forget to water it.

MAKE FAUX PLANTS LOOK FABULOUS

Your secret's safe with us — and if you abide by our suggestions, no one else will ever know your gorgeous greenery isn't alive.

Add moss.
Buy the decorative kind, and pad the top of the planter with it for added natural texture.

Bend the stems.
Place individual blooms in a vase, then bend and twist stems outward to mimic the movement of live flowers, which face the sun.

Cut single branches.
To make one artificial plant go further, snip off its leafy stems and scatter them in bud vases on small shelves and windowsills.

Keep them clean.
All leaves, real or not, attract dust. When you do your weekly cleaning, run a damp rag or microfiber cloth over the petals and leaves to wipe dust away.

ARRANGE FLOWERS

Our advice works whether you're bringing blooms in from your garden (see page 156 for how to grow perennials) or perking up a bouquet from the grocery store.

Create a grid with transparent tape to keep flowers in place in a shallow vase. First, make a grid with clear water-resistant floral tape (or thin transparent tape) to hold flowers in place. Then insert fuller flowers at an angle since they'll take up the most room. Next, use medium-size flowers to fill in the remaining holes in the arrangement and the smallest florals as your accents to finish the design.

Stack a vase within a vase in order to layer fruit slices along the inside. Find a vase that fits inside another vase with ¹/₂ inch of room between them. Fill up the space between the two vases most of the way with water before slipping in sliced lemons. Pop your accent flowers in the center vase.

Dry flowers by hanging them upside down in a cool space. Tie the ends of the stems with a ribbon and hang them from a nail, the corner of a picture frame or a key rack, where they'll serve as decoration.

Make a rose twist bouquet with crisscrossing stems. Start by inserting your first stem into the vase, and then place the next stem across it and continue crossing each new stem over the last one until the glass is full.

Use a teacup as a vase for flowers with shorter stems. Keep the stems together using a clear hair tie so they don't separate in the teacup, which also makes it easier to change the water.

EXTEND THE LIFE OF YOUR BLOOMS

Cut flower stems at a 45-degree angle 1 inch from the bottom. This instantly increases the surface area for water intake so your flowers will be well hydrated.

Add a vodka-sugar elixir to your water to keep flowers looking flawless longer. Before putting your flowers in a vase, add several drops of sugar-free vodka and a teaspoon of white sugar, which delays wilting. When your flowers eventually do start to die, add a shot of sugar-free vodka to the water; the stems will stand up straight again for a day or two.

Drop a penny in your vase to keep your flower water fresh longer. The copper in pennies works as an acidifier, which helps prevent fungus or bacteria. Pennies minted before 1982 contain more copper, so opt for those to keep your arrangement looking amazing a couple of days longer.

GROW an INDOOR HERB GARDEN

Flavor your favorite soups, vegetables, roasts and more with a never-ending supply of fresh-picked leaves. For best growth, place your herbs in a spot that gets at least 6 hours of sun daily. In addition to sunlight, all herbs need to be planted in pots with good drainage. If you're concerned that the drainage holes will ruin your tabletop or windowsill, use a saucer or liner to catch any excess water. For specifics on what to grow, follow this guide. For tips on storing fresh herbs after picking, see page 28.

HERBS	GROWING TIPS	USE
Basil	**Start basil from seeds,** and place the pots in a south-facing window; it likes lots of sun and warmth plus ample water, so keep the soil moist but not drenched. Pinch the tops of the plant frequently to encourage fuller growth.	**Add to** pizza and pasta sauces, ratatouille and salads. **Puree any extra leaves** with a little water, then pour into an ice cube tray and freeze to use later in sauces, soups and pesto (see page 40 for our recipe).
Chives	**This oniony herb** does quite nicely in a container with full sun. One of the easiest herbs to grow indoors, chives are ready to be chopped when they reach 6 to 12 inches.	**Mince the leaves,** and then sprinkle them in soups and salads or on top of eggs or baked potatoes. **Use the edible** purple flowers as garnishes.
Mint	**All mint varieties** prefer a cool, moist spot in partial shade but will also grow in full sun. Most mint plants spread rampantly, so always plant it in its own container.	**Stir into tea** (hot or iced). **Add chopped** fresh leaves to lamb, rice, salads and cooked vegetables. **Drop a leaf** into a cocktail.

HERBS	GROWING TIPS	USE
Parsley	**Start parsley from seeds,** or dig up a clump from your garden at the end of the season. Parsley likes full sun but will grow slowly in an east- or west-facing window.	**Choose the** flat-leaf variety for cooking and the curly kind for pretty garnishes on potatoes, rice, fish, lamb and steak.
Rosemary	**Start with** a cutting of rosemary, and keep it in a moist soilless mix until it roots. It grows best in a south-facing window with good drainage. Prune regularly (up to a third of the plant).	**Dry extra stems** to flavor winter stews and soups. **Freshen the air** — the pungent scent of this herb acts like a natural air freshener.
Sage	**Take a tip** that was cut from an outdoor plant to start an indoor sage plant. It tolerates dry, indoor air well but needs the strong sun from a south-facing window. You'll be rewarded with gorgeous silver foliage and a nice aroma.	**Add to poultry,** pork or sausage dishes, as well as Thanksgiving turkey and stuffing. (See pages 194–199 for more tips about Turkey Day.)
Thyme	**Root a soft tip** that was cut from an outdoor plant, or dig up and repot the entire thing. Thyme likes full sun but will grow in an east- or west-facing window. Keep the soil moist, and harvest sprigs as needed.	**Add fresh** or dried leaves to roasts, sauces, soups and dressings — or infuse them in butter or oil. **Dry thyme** leaves by cutting whole stems and tying them into bunches. Hang in a dry, airy location out of the sun.

LAB TIP The essential oils of herbs are at their most powerful early in the morning, so that's the best time to harvest. Make sure to pick a mixture of leaves — old, new, large, small— to ensure continued growth.

UPGRADE YOUR HOME GYM

Having a dedicated place to work out can help motivate and inspire you.

Stock a sturdy basket.
Opt for one that stands up on its own and can fit a few rolled-up mats, a yoga block and workout bands.

Install storage cubbies or shelves.
Keep rolled towels, cycling shoes, water bottles and hair ties within reach by storing them neatly in a cubby or on a floating shelf. Small, clear stackable bins can also help keep gear orderly.

Lay down padded flooring.
If you have the space, interlocking mat tiles can help protect the floor (and your knees).

Add a full-length mirror.
This not only helps make your space look bigger but also allows you to keep an eye on your form. If space is tight, hang one on the wall or behind a door.

Get inspired.
Turn the walls into an uplifting focal point by adding a bold paint color, statement art or an inspiring quote that will encourage you. Add a lamp or strip lights, and consider a wall mount or holder for your smartphone or tablet.

CLEAN YOUR YOGA MAT
Depending on the intensity of your sessions, you can usually go a week or so before your mat needs a good wipe-down. If you sweat a lot or the mat retains an odor, clean it more often, though some mat makers caution that overcleaning can cause the mats to wear out more quickly. Here's how to do it:

Spot-clean both sides of your mat with either a yoga mat cleaner (some mat makers sell these cleaners too) or a few drops of mild dishwashing liquid mixed with two cups of warm water in a spray bottle. Spritz the solution onto the mat, and wipe the surfaces clean with a soft cloth. Rinse the mat with a damp cloth that you've dipped in clear water and wrung well. Lay the mat flat or hang it over a shower rod to dry fully before rolling it back up.

PLAN YOUR PERFECT HOME OFFICE

Just about anyone can benefit from having a functional workspace to tackle a to-do list, make headway on a creative project or simply catch up on some emails. Luckily, when it comes to home office design schemes, the possibilities are endless.

Carve out a nook.
Consider setting up in a corner of the kitchen, under the stairs or in an unused closet. Decorate it like you would any other room: Add wallpaper, light fixtures and thoughtful touches.

Illuminate your space.
Home offices are usually the smallest room in the house, often lacking large windows, so they tend not to get an abundance of natural light. Use a task light when you're working to ensure you don't strain your eyes, and mirrors to make the most of whatever light you have.

Get playful.
It is, after all, an office in your home, so bring in accessories that speak to you — rugs, cushions, mementoes, candles or a reed diffuser.

Think beyond the desk.
Expand your workspace by adding a sleek wooden shelf at eye level. The rest is up to you: Display artwork, or use the shelf as a handy storage spot for gadgets.

Go for an unconventional desk.
If you're short on space, stick a console table against a blank wall for a makeshift office. Hang a framed bulletin board directly above the workspace for added inspiration.

Coordinate the rug and curtains.
Even if you opt for a muted paint, infuse color into your space with a patterned rug and coordinating drapery. Then dress up the room with decorative accents in the same hue.

Define the space with color.
Spruce up an all-white bedroom by weaving a pop of color, like a resonant magenta, into your closet office setup. Pull the look together with a statement piece of art.

LAB TIP Use toolbox organizers to keep everything in its place and prevent tools from getting lost or damaged.

CHAPTER 4

MAINTAIN & REPAIR

STOCK YOUR TOOLBOX

Here are the 11 tools everyone should have in their kit: You know what they say— use the right tool for the job.

Masking Tape
Easy to tear, easy to remove and endlessly useful for indicating whatever you need to hammer, cut, paint, donate, replace or refurbish.

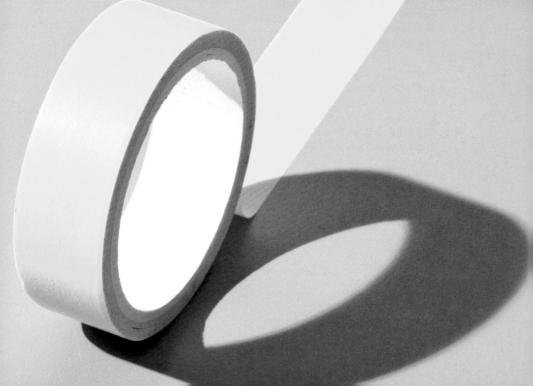

Cordless Drill

Newer models are available with stud finders, making hanging or mounting projects a snap.

Hammer

While there are plenty of fancy hammers, old school works just fine. Use the claw side to remove nails.

Safety Goggles

Nails slip, old paint chips go flying. These should be nonnegotiable when working on home-improvement projects.

Utility Knife

Also known as a box cutter, this knife can fold out or push up.

Drain Snake

Run this thin plastic tool down your sink whenever water drains more slowly than usual.

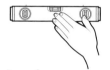

Level

You can eyeball whether something is straight or even, but only a level will tell you for sure. You could also try a level app on your phone.

Screwdrivers

Buy an assortment — slotted, Phillips, star, square — and you'll be able to secure every kind of screw.

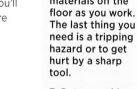

TIPS FOR ANY PROJECT

1. Think through every job beforehand, and try to make one run for supplies.

2. Keep tools, hardware and materials off the floor as you work. The last thing you need is a tripping hazard or to get hurt by a sharp tool.

3. Put everything in its place at the end of each session. Your work area should be restored to a pre-project level of orderliness.

Flashlight

It helps when the power goes out, of course, but a flashlight is also useful for peering into crevices and corners.

Pencil

Sticking a pencil behind your ear will make you feel handier and readier to tackle any project. It's also helpful for marking or noting measurements.

Tape Measure

Measure twice, cut once.

SOLVE PROBLEMS with UNEXPECTED HOUSEHOLD SUPPLIES

Before calling a repair person, check whether one of these ordinary objects can be put to an extraordinary use.

Aluminum Foil

A ball of aluminum foil can help scrub cookware like glass casserole dishes or cast-iron skillets. It can also be used to wrap the feet of your couch to help scoot it across carpeting (but avoid using this trick on delicate surfaces or furniture that could be scratched by the foil).

Clear Nail Polish

Apply a drop of clear nail polish to a hanging thread or a button's center. Once it's dry, the polish will prevent the stitches from fraying over time.

Cooking Spray

Spritz a little cooking spray on a squeaky door hinge. Then swing the door back and forth to work the spray in and quiet the creaking.

Duct Tape

Duct tape's super-stickiness removes other stubborn adhesive leftovers, especially on glass. Place a piece over the offending spot, rub it a few times and peel the mess away. Finish off with a window cleaner.

Newspapers

Next time a glass shatters on your kitchen floor, pick up the large pieces and then dampen a piece of newspaper. Blot the smaller shards, and they'll lift right up.

Rubber Band

Stretch one end of a rubber band over the top of an open paint can and use it to wipe excess paint from the brush. With its edges kept clean, the can will be a breeze to seal back up.

Soda-Can Tab

Expand your closet's clothing capacity by repurposing a soda-can tab: Slip one end over a hanger's hook, then suspend a second hanger from the tab's other end.

Toothpaste

Use a little squirt of regular white toothpaste (not gel) to clean silver, faucets, dirty sneakers, makeup-smeared counters and tea- or coffee-stained mugs. To remove strong smells, such as garlic and fish, from your hands, rub in a smear of toothpaste, then rinse.

SCAN ME!
5 CLEVER WAYS TO USE ALUMINUM FOIL

The Daily News

ENHANCE YOUR HOME in a WEEKEND

These small-scale home repairs can be done in 48 hours and deliver big results.

1 Carpet Dent
Put an ice cube in each indentation, and let the cubes slowly melt. Wait 12 hours, blot up wet spots, then use the edge of a spoon to lift the carpet fibers back up. Need a quicker fix? Blast the dents with a burst of steam from an iron or garment steamer. The appliance should not touch the carpet, but it should be held close enough that the fibers heat up and relax. Then fluff with your fingers.

2 Dent in the Wall
Wedge a wad of newspaper into the dent, leaving about a $1/4$-inch gap between the paper and the rim of the hole. Use a putty knife to fill the gap with joint compound, then smooth it with the blade or rub it down with a fine-grain sandpaper. Let the compound dry for 24 hours, then paint over the spot.

3 Holes in the Wall
Little holes made by common nails can be filled and don't require sanding. Place spackle on the edge of your putty knife, and hold the knife at a 45-degree angle to the wall. Drag across the hole in a smooth, solid motion, repeating if necessary to ensure the patch is smooth with the wall. Larger holes could require the use of mesh tape or a wall repair patch. Apply the tape or patch over the hole, spackle, and sand the area down until the finish is smooth with the surrounding wall.

4 Running Toilet
Lift off the tank's lid and take a look. If water is overflowing into the vertical tube, you'll need to lower the water level in the tank. To do so, simply bend the arm on the float downward or, in newer models, squeeze the adjustment clips and slide the float down. If the water level isn't the problem, add a little food coloring to the tank and wait about 20 minutes. A change in color in the toilet bowl means the flapper — a rubber diaphragm at the bottom of the tank — is leaking and needs to be replaced. Turn off the water supply behind the toilet, and pop out the flapper with your hands. Take it to a hardware store, and ask for a replacement. The new one should pop back in the same way.

5 Weird Smells
An odd smell may be due to mold or mildew growth brought about by excessive humidity; food for the fungi to form on (old books, paper, junk, carpet, dirt); darkness; and/or lack of air circulation. Solve the excessive moisture in the air by using a dehumidifier, opening a window or plugging leaks, and go from there. And see page 129 for advice about conquering mold and for cleaning info.

SPIFF UP YOUR FURNITURE

The benefits of fixing your furniture are great: you'll save money, increase your knowledge of how things work, preserve an heirloom, help protect the environment, and enhance your sense of pride and ownership.

Busted Handles

When the screw holes in wooden handles are stripped, you won't be able to tighten the handle no matter how hard you try. Fill the holes with drillable wood putty (check the label), so the screws have something to bite into. Once the putty is dry, drill a pilot hole and reattach the handle using a screw.

Candle and Crayon Stains

Candle wax and crayon respond well to ice. Fill a plastic bag with ice cubes, wrap it in a towel, and place it on the stain until it hardens (a few minutes), then carefully coax wax off with a plastic spatula.

Dented Wooden Furniture

Dampen a large cotton dishtowel, fold it into quarters, and place it over the ding. Set your iron to high (without steam), and press the cloth a few seconds (making sure the iron doesn't touch the wood) until the water from the towel stops steaming. If the grain is still a little dented, repeat. Follow up with a coat of furniture polish on the entire tabletop. This process works for white rings too.

Saggy Sofa

If the upholstery is still in good shape, remove the foam insert and take it to a craft store, where you can get a replacement cut to fit. Flip cushions every few months to help them wear evenly.

Uneven Table

Fasten nail-on glides to the ends of the legs. They're designed to keep the legs from scuffing the floor, but they can also be used to level a table. Measure the gap between the short leg and the floor. Next, drill a pilot hole and insert a glide in the three nonproblem legs. Wedge washers into the fourth leg to get the right height, then add the glide.

Wobbly Chair

Unscrew the wobbly piece. Stick in a toothpick (or two) where the leg meets the seat, and secure the pieces with a little glue. When it dries, break off the excess toothpick, and replace the screw (the toothpicks help anchor the screw). Use wood touch-up markers for scratches.

> **LAB TIP** Create a just-in-case fund. Try to save 1% of your home's value each year for unexpected repairs. You may be surprised at what some insurance plans don't cover (like floods and the failure of items because of age).

Avoid Big Problems
with Small Appliances

1 **Ask about
hand-me-downs.**
Do some due diligence
before accepting a previ-
ously used device to find
out its history. For example, a well-loved blender
being given away by
someone who's upgrad-
ing is a great way to stay
green. But a blender that's
been in someone's garage
for years might have got-
ten wet or been damaged.
See our tips on page 68
for how to safely dispose
of (practically) everything.

2 **Inspect wires.**
If you notice that
an item's cord is frayed
or that there are exposed
wires from normal wear
and tear (or nibbling
pests), toss it. You don't
want to risk fire or elec-
trocution.

3 **Remember
to unplug.**
Get into the habit of
unplugging everything,
from your toaster oven to
your slow cooker, when
you aren't using it. The
risk of a spontaneous fire
is very low, but not zero.

FIX YOUR APPLIANCES

We diagnosed some common problems
and came up with easy solutions.

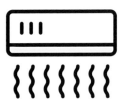

APPLIANCE	Air Conditioner		Washing Machine		
ISSUE	AC isn't cooling		Washing machine is leaking	Washing machine smells musty	
LIKELY CULPRIT	Blocked filter	Compressor issue	Cracked water hose	Too much detergent	Mold or mildew
SOLUTIONS	A filthy indoor air filter may block enough air to cut cooling performance. Replace it with a clean, new, appropriately sized filter.	The system's refrigerant charge is low or an outdoor compressor/condenser may need to be cleaned, is shot or needs a new fan motor. Call an AC repair person.	Turn off the water supply, then replace the hose (this universal part should screw back in).	Opt for the most high-efficiency brand of detergent, and limit the amount to about two tablespoons. Skip the fabric softener, which tends to "stick" in the washing machine.	Run a cycle with just hot water and bleach.
PREVENTION	Regular maintenance will help reduce problems.			Wipe down the inside of your machine after each use, and leave the door ajar.	

Dryer

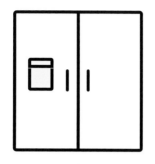

Fridge

Garbage Disposal

Clothes aren't drying (dryer is taking too long)	Fridge isn't cold enough	Garbage disposal won't work

Clogged vent / lint buildup	A breaker is off	Loose gasket (door seal)	Dirty coils	Power is off	Clog
Unplug the machine, and clear lint and debris from the vent and the back of the dryer using a special brush snake or your vacuum cleaner hose.	Make sure both breakers are on. Dryers typically have two, and if only one trips, the dryer can still run without drying the clothes.	Clean the gasket. If it's not sealing properly, cool air may be escaping. Use warm soapy water and rinse and dry well.	Clean the coils. They're generally located below or behind the fridge. Unplug the fridge, pop off the grate (if coils are below), and use your vacuum cleaner hose with crevice attachment.	Check the power.	Run ice cubes through the disposal, which will dislodge the clog. Use an Allen wrench (most disposals come with one, which fits in a hole under the unit) to get it turning again.

Clear the filter after every use and get yearly maintenance and a deep cleaning from a professional, which will help your machine function and reduce the risk of fire.

Regular cleaning can lower your energy bill, since your fridge will operate more efficiently.

WINTERIZE YOUR HOME

Prepare your house and your things,
then grab a hot chocolate and let it snow.

1 **Drain water out of garden hoses and stow them inside.** Otherwise, the water can freeze, weaken the lining and cause holes. You can also shut off the water valve, usually a brass, lever-style handle located in your basement or crawl space near the faucet. Turn it until it doesn't move, about 90 degrees. Open the faucet outside until remaining water drips out. Some faucets have an indoor drain (capped by a small cover); let water out of there too.

2 **Keep pipes warm.** During long cold snaps, open cabinets a crack to let warmer indoor air reach the pipes. Or slip foam insulation sleeves over pipes that you can access. If a pipe is frozen, open the faucet and direct a hairdryer toward the icy section.

3 **Cover firewood with a tarp.** Keep stacks of firewood at least 20 feet from the house, as mice like to nest in the piles. Burn only dry, seasoned wood. Wood that hasn't been properly seasoned or dried will smoke heavily when you try to light it. You can buy seasoned wood, or you can season it yourself by stacking freshly cut logs into outdoor piles. It takes about six months for wood to become properly seasoned.

4 **Seal gaps and cracks in your foundation and walls.** Fill larger openings with an expanding foam filler (the foam can be painted, sanded and stained). Use a paintable caulk around windows and doors. It should stay soft, so you can peel it off easily if you make mistakes.

POSITION GUTTERS AND DOWN-SPOUTS

The best way to make sure your gutters are draining away from your foundation is to watch them in action. Head outside the next time it rains and pay attention. Check out the gaps between the downspouts and drainage pipes. If necessary, add a length of downspout or a splash block so that water from your gutters is directed at least 4 to 6 feet away from your foundation.

Be a Draft Detective

Find where cold air is coming in.

COMMON DRAFTY AREAS

- Attic hatches
- Baseboards
- Cable TV and phone lines
- Door and window frames
- Electrical outlets
- Fireplace dampers
- Switch plates
- Vents and fans
- Wall- or window-mounted air conditioners

1 Switch on a flashlight.

At night, shine a flashlight on door and window frames. If the person on the other side sees light through any cracks, you may have a leak.

2 Grab a dollar bill.

If you think doors are to blame, slip a dollar bill (or standard piece of paper) under the door. If you can pull the dollar bill out without it dragging, then you have a significant air leak.

3 Light a candle.

Turn off the furnace and water heater, and turn on exhaust fans. Move the lit candle slowly around the perimeter. The flame will flicker near a leak.

4 Use a thermal leak detector.

This device reads the surface temperatures of walls, doors, floorboards and more. If the reading is a lot colder than the air, there's a leak.

GET RID OF DRAFTS

For cracks less than ¼ inch, use a long-lasting caulk. In general, look for caulks made with mold-free technology that adhere to common surfaces.

LAB TIP
As a rule of thumb, you'll need to buy a tube of caulk for every two windows or doors that need sealing.

For cracks between ¼ inch and 3 inches, use spray foam. Unlike caulk, spray foam can be more difficult to use, so we recommend dispensing it onto newspaper before tackling trouble areas. To quicken the curing process — the time it takes to settle — mist the area with water before and after spraying.

For invisible leaks, check your insulation. If the insulation in your attic doesn't reach the top of the floor joists, there's not enough to trap heat. Visit a home-improvement store for DIY attic insulation, or hire someone to get the job done.

PREVENT WATER DAMAGE

Left untreated, even the smallest water damage can cause mold growth, water contamination, structural problems, damaged wiring, odors, stains — the list goes on and on. The best way to avoid water damage is to make sure it doesn't happen in the first place.

Upgrade to reinforced hoses. Replace the supply hoses on your appliances. Stainless steel versions are stronger and longer-lasting.

Replace your gutters. Overflowing gutters cause water to spill over and drip into the walls and basement of your house. Opt for a curved gutter with built-in hood, which will save you from cleaning the gutters ever again and helps prevent clogs from built-up debris, to reduce your risk of water damage.

Be careful about what and where you plant. Tree roots can be aggressive, bumping into or dislodging underground pipes, septic tanks and sprinkler lines. Roots can also cause damage to the foundation, which can lead to water damage. The maximum distance of a plant's height and width is the same that you should leave for the roots.

Install a sump pump. Basements are the first place to flood when a big storm hits, so if you live in a rainy climate, invest in a sump pump to prevent basement flooding. These devices pump water rising up from the ground back to the outside so your basement and the rest of your home stay dry.

Take good care of your pipes. Use a drain snake instead of unclogging chemicals when a sink starts to back up. Liquid can corrode pipes. Never pour grease or oil down the drain. You know how leftover oil congeals and hardens in the pan after you cook? That's also what happens to it in your pipes.

LAB TIP Do a manual leak audit. Examine any appliance that uses water, from your washer to your ice maker to your shower. Look for damaged rubber tubing or loose fittings, and check the surrounding area — including the ceilings and walls in rooms below bathrooms, kitchens and laundry rooms — for water stains, cracked pipes and mold.

CLEAR the AIR

Sealing your house keeps cold air out, but it also keeps stale air in, possibly triggering allergies, asthma and other health problems. Proper ventilation, including running your range hood when cooking and periodically cracking open a window, will help, as will regular dusting and vacuuming (check out our tips for speed-cleaning on page 46). Here are other steps you can take to keep yourself healthy and your home smelling fresh.

GET YOUR HOME TESTED FOR RADON

Nearly one in every 15 homes in the U.S. is estimated to have elevated radon levels, says the EPA. Radon, a naturally occurring invisible and odorless radioactive gas — the leading cause of cancer in nonsmokers — travels up through ground soil into your home's air. It's not always limited to any geographic area, so even if your neighbor's radon level is low, that doesn't mean your home is clear. All homes should be tested for radon at least once. You can purchase a testing kit, or hire a certified radon professional to administer tests.

1 Use the back burner.
Tests done by the Berkeley Lab found that pollutants were extracted from the air at a higher rate by exhaust fans when food was cooked on back burners.

2 Heat on medium.
Cooking at high temperatures creates more air pollutants, so opt for medium- or low-heat techniques, such as slow-cooking, baking, sautéing, simmering and steaming, and avoid frying foods.

3 Use an air purifier.
Nab dust, pollen and smoke from cooking or candles with an air purifier that has an AHAM Verifide Mark from the Association of Home Appliance Manufacturers. Also make sure it has the right clean air delivery rate (CADR) for your room size (most list square footage on the packaging or website).

4 Refresh carpets and rugs.
Sprinkle baking soda all over the carpet — not just problem areas — and let sit for a few hours before vacuuming. The same method works for pet beds and mattresses.

5 Go green.
Aloe vera is one of the best air-purifying plants you can buy as it continuously releases oxygen while simultaneously taking in carbon dioxide. It's also relatively easy to maintain and particularly forgiving of forgetful waterers.

SAY GOODBYE to INDOOR ALLERGENS

Indoor allergens can bring on similar miseries to their outdoor brethren — a stuffy or runny nose; watery, itchy eyes; fatigue; and breathing trouble — but can be harder to escape. These tips will help when dealing with common offenders.

Dust Mites

These are tiny arthropods (like spiders) that feed off the skin we shed every day — and they usually nest in fabrics, especially bedding. When laundering, use hot water and high heat. An allergen-proof casing on your mattress and pillows could help as well. If you have carpeting or rugs, clean them weekly with a vacuum that has a high-efficiency particulate air (HEPA) filter.

Mold

Mold and mildew often develop in moist areas, such as damp bathrooms and basements, or places near water leaks. The fungi spores can travel through the air and cause issues when you breathe them in. That's why it's important to get those damp areas cleaned and address the root cause of mold. Dehumidifiers can help, but make sure to clean out the water they collect a few times a week. See page 131 for more advice about removing mold and mildew.

Pests

To make sure there's nothing around to entice pests such as mice and cockroaches, keep food in sealed containers, wipe up crumbs, cover trash cans and clean dirty dishes. See page 136 for more tips about preventing pests.

Pet Dander

Dander includes pet dandruff, which can trigger allergies. If Fido or Fifi might be causing your sneezes, try vacuuming more frequently, bathing your pet weekly and placing HEPA purifiers throughout your home. Give your hands a good washing after a cuddle, petting or playing session too.

DISSOLVE HARD-WATER STAINS

Unsightly residue can appear when droplets dry and leave behind white deposits of calcium and magnesium. These minerals clog faucets and showers and make crystal look cloudy. A fast solution: vinegar!

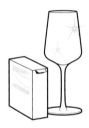  

Get sparkling glasses

With hard water, even washing by hand can leave glasses spotty. To erase the marks, heat some white vinegar in the microwave on High until it's warm. Pour the vinegar into a plastic basin and immerse the glasses for 10 minutes, turning them to cover all sides. Remove them and generously sprinkle on baking soda, rub gently with your fingers, rinse and buff dry.

Polish faucets

If chrome fixtures have lost their luster or, worse, are down to a drip, you can renew them. Dip a cloth in a 50/50 mixture of white vinegar and water, wrap it around the stained area, and leave it for up to 10 minutes, then rinse and buff dry. Repeat if needed. If there's an aerator (a removable screen), unscrew it and soak it in vinegar, then scrub it to restore the flow.

De-gunk showerheads

A wimpy shower stream is one of the clearest signs that you have a hard-water problem. There's often buildup on the nozzle too. To clean, dip a toothbrush in white vinegar and scrub the water jets. Wipe, then turn on the shower to blast the jets open. You can also soak the showerhead in vinegar, but be careful — doing this can damage gold, brass, or nickel-coated finishes.

LAB TIP You can prevent your drains from getting clogged by regularly using a homemade vinegar solution. Mix $1/2$ cup baking soda with $1/4$ cup table salt. Pour the mixture down the drain and follow with 1 cup heated vinegar. It will likely foam. Let stand for 15 minutes and follow by running hot tap water for 15 to 30 seconds.

Remove Mold and Mildew

Whether you call it mold or mildew, this fungus thrives in warm, wet conditions and can aggravate allergies. Act quickly to keep it from spreading.

Surface Mold

Bathroom-tile grout and painted walls are common areas where mold grows. Mild stains can be scrubbed with a grout cleaner, a mold remover or a bleach-and-water solution. Wear rubber gloves and eye protection, and use products according to label directions. For small spots on painted walls and ceilings, mix ³/₄ cup of chlorine bleach in a gallon of warm water. Apply to the stains with a sponge or a brush. Let sit 5 minutes, then scrub, rinse and air-dry.

Fabric Mold

Wet towels on the floor, forgotten gym clothes in a bag and linens stored in a damp basement are prime breeding grounds for mold. When you see those black spots, take the affected items outside and brush away as much as you can. Then rub in liquid laundry detergent and wash items with fabric-safe bleach in the hottest water that's safe. To keep the stain from setting, avoid the dryer until you know the mold is gone.

LAB TIP
Severe mold could be the sign of a bigger problem. Call in a pro to have it safely removed.

HONOR YOUR HEIRLOOMS

Care for your treasures to ensure that you can pass them on to the next generation.

Antique Brass

If you own antique brass, be especially careful about cleaning it. You could inadvertently reduce the value by rubbing off its lovely old surface patina. To clean, simply remove dirt and dust with a microfiber cloth. Polishing tends to use abrasives, so every time tarnish forms and is polished away, part of the original surface is lost. Do this too often and you could lose detail or even hallmarks. If the item is truly tarnished, check with a professional.

China

Avoiding storage mistakes will protect your pieces and keep them at the ready for the next special event. When returning fine china to the cabinet, place an inexpensive paper plate or round coffee filter between the dishes to prevent chips and nicks. Then cover the whole stack with plastic wrap or plastic dry-cleaning bags so the china will stay clean.

Jewelry

This solution works for silver, gold and most precious stones: mix $1/2$ teaspoon mild dish-washing soap, $1/2$ teaspoon ammonia and 1 cup water. Soak your items for 3 to 5 minutes. Brush with a soft toothbrush, and dry with a microfiber or terrycloth towel. Do not use this solution on pearls or "soft" stones like opals and lapis. Wrap each piece individually in a soft velvet pouch; that way, hard stones like diamonds and sapphires won't scratch the softer ones.

Silver

To make silver shine you'll need polish.

1. **Put a small amount of silver polish** on a clean cloth, dampened if directed. Any soft cloth will do.

2. **Rub the polish** on your item in an up-and-down motion, to avoid highlighting fine scratches.

3. **Turn the cloth** frequently as you work, to avoid spreading tarnish.

4. **Rinse in warm water** and buff with a clean, dry cloth to shine.

PREVENT TARNISH

Store each piece of silver in its own anti-tarnish bag or felt-lined box in a cool, dry spot.

Add a piece of chalk in an anti-tarnish bag to help remove moisture from the air.

Put jewelry on after perfume to prevent it from sticking to your silver.

Don't be afraid to wear your silver: Friction slows down tarnishing, which means the more you wear it, the more it'll shine.

MAKE YOUR OWN SILVER CLEANER

Without a doubt, targeted silver polish is the most effective way to clean silver. But if you're in a pinch, you can turn to your pantry for homemade remedies.

For silver that is dull, filmy or not yet discolored, mix a few drops of mild dish soap with warm water and dip in a soft cloth. Rub the jewelry, then rinse in cool water and buff with a cloth until dry.

For silver that is heavily tarnished, mix a paste of three parts baking soda to one part water. Wet the silver and apply the cleaner with a soft, lint-free cloth (avoid using paper towels). Work the paste into the crevices, turning the cloth as it gets gray. Rinse and buff dry.

EMERGENCY-PROOF YOUR LIFE

Disasters are inevitable. The best way to defend yourself against any emergency is to be prepared.

Know what to expect.
Find out which disasters your town, state and region are most at risk for, and plan accordingly. Sign up for emergency alerts.

Make an action plan.
Designate two meeting places for your household (one close by and one a little farther away in your neighborhood), and hang a map with those spots marked near your emergency kit.

Prepare your house.
Unplug appliances and electronics and turn off air conditioners, whether you stay or go. This will prevent damage when the electricity surges back on. Leave one lamp on so you'll know when the power's back. If water lines could be affected, you'll want to fill your tub and turn off the line. Use this water for sanitation like handwashing and pouring down the toilet to flush it.

Stock your pantry.
If you'll be inside for a while, weather the storm with high-protein, plant-based shelf-stable items. See our recommendations for a well-stocked pantry on page 14.

Return safely.
Coming home after a major disaster can be daunting. Take proper precautions such as these:

- **Look for damage outside,** especially loose or fallen power cables, damaged gas lines, and cracks in the foundation or in beams. If you have trees nearby, carefully assess their stability.

- **Note sounds and odors.** If you smell gas or hear a hissing noise, call the fire department and have them inspect the situation before you reenter.

- **Check inside.** If the power is still out, use a flashlight (not a candle — open flames can burn items or cause gases to ignite) to assess damage.

- **Inspect appliances.** For small appliances like coffeemakers and toasters, look closely at the cords for fraying or exposed wires before using them again. Fridges, ranges and washers can be more complicated; call a service company to check the safety of connections and components, then replace anything that's severely damaged.

- **Document the damage.** It may be hard emotionally, but if you want to file an insurance claim, you'll need a visual record with clear pictures and thorough notes before you clean up.

Pack an Emergency Preparedness Kit

Packing a go-kit — tools and supplies that can sustain your family and keep you relatively comfortable in case of a crisis — is an integral part of any disaster preparedness plan. Having a disaster survival kit in your home doesn't make you a doomsday prepper, just smart.

BASIC SUPPLIES TO KEEP IN YOUR KIT

- Enough water for three days (aim for at least a gallon of water per person per day)

- Reusable water bottles

- Enough food for three days. Aim for a selection of nonperishable, high-protein foods.

- Mess kits with plates, bowls, cups and sporks

- First aid essentials like pain meds and antibacterial cream

- A crank-powered radio

- Duct tape

- A headlamp or portable lighting

- A reusable phone charger

- Lightweight, waterproof blankets

- Miscellaneous hygiene supplies like N95 masks, disinfectant wipes, hand sanitizer, diapers and tampons

- Waterproof matches and/or fire starters

- A whistle

- Extra batteries

- Pet food, medication and other essential supplies

- A waterproof bag of important documents and money, including a paper map of your area, your and your family's passports, bank account records, insurance policies, a paper list of phone numbers and addresses of friends and family, and medical and prescription information

- A multiuse tool — the best ones come with everything from scissors and a can opener to pliers and screwdrivers

LAB TIP Consider posting a yearly reminder in your family calendar so you can make sure everything is still unexpired and up-to-date.

PREVENT PESTS

The best way to banish pests is to prevent them from entering your home in the first place.

Keep your kitchen tidy. Wipe down kitchen surfaces, clean up spilled food and throw away uneaten pet food to prevent unwanted visitors.

Contain your food. Some bugs feed on dried food, while other critters are partial to any food items you leave unsealed. Seal up all open food packages in airtight food containers.

Close your trash can and take out your recycling. Look for an airtight lid or use rubber cords to keep it shut. Mice will munch on paper and cardboard, and silverfish and cockroaches can burrow in magazines and newspapers.

Drive out the damp. Open windows and keep kitchens and bathrooms ventilated, preventing any bug breeding grounds.

Watch out for pests on your pets. Once a week, vacuum areas used by pets with a strong-suction vacuum, and shake out and wash your pet bedding once every two weeks.

Spray — don't stomp. It's always best to use a dedicated household insecticide spray or sprinkle an insecticide powder. Stomping on cockroaches can spread their eggs.

Store clean clothes. Make sure your clothes are laundered and free of stains before putting them away for the season. Soiled clothes can attract clothes moths, carpet beetles, silverfish, crickets and other insects.

Use caulk and steel wool to seal up the house. Mice can fit through openings the size of a dime, and they'll gnaw to make the opening larger. Plug up any holes you see — especially around pipes and basement foundations — with steel wool and caulk. Seal gaps around doors and windows, where utility lines enter your home, and beneath or on top of sinks as well.

Prune shrubbery away from your house. Shrubbery and branches are basically inviting mice and insects into your home, so cut shrubbery back from the exterior of your house.

BANISH BUGS and RODENTS

Here's how to get rid of the most common insects and pests.

PEST	SOLUTIONS
Ants	**Dust infested areas** inside with boric acid mixed with an equal amount of flour, cornmeal or sugar — the ants will carry the grains back to the nest, feed on them and die. (Keep pets and kids away from treated areas, since boric acid and borax powder are toxic.)
Bedbugs	**Wash and dry** infested bedding and clothing at the hottest temperature they can withstand. While some bugs will die in the washing machine, it's the heat of the dryer that will kill more of them. Run the dryer for at least an hour. **Vacuum** skirting boards and sleeping areas, and dispose of the vacuum bag immediately.
Moths	**Vacuum** and then dispose of the vacuum bag immediately (as it may contain eggs). **For pantry moths**, throw out any potentially contaminated food immediately. **Scrub shelves** and walls thoroughly.
Cock-roaches	**Cut off** their food supply. **Eliminate** hiding places.
Drain Flies	**Use a drain cleaner** to get rid of the bacteria, sewage and gunk in your drain or toilet.
Fleas	**Vacuum the floors**, furniture, and anything your pet is around daily. **Seal and dispose** of the vacuum bag afterwards. **Steam clean** carpets to kill lingering fleas.
Fungus Gnats	**Repot houseplants** in new soil, then go easy on watering.
Mice	**Find their entry point** and set traps. Peanut butter is a favorite lure.

DIY FRUIT FLY TRAPS

Paper Cone and Fruit
Place a little vinegar and a small chunk of ripe fruit in a jar. Roll a piece of paper into a cone and stick it into the jar, narrow opening downward. Fruit flies will be drawn in but won't be able to get out.

Apple Cider Vinegar
Remove the cap from the bottle (it doesn't have to be full). Cover the opening with plastic wrap and secure with a rubber band. Then poke a hole for fruit flies to enter.

Vinegar and Dish Soap
Add three drops of dish soap to a bowl of vinegar and leave it uncovered. The soap cuts the surface tension of the vinegar so the flies will sink and drown.

LAB TIP Wipe down garden tools after every use to keep them rust-free, sharp, and working their best.

CHAPTER 5

ENJOY the OUTDOORS

ADD CURB APPEAL

Keeping the outside of your house looking clean, neat and manicured helps make your property a place you're proud to come home to. These seven upgrades will refresh your home's exterior, both cosmetically and functionally.

Redo the front door.
Consider repainting, or even just replacing the hardware, including the handle and numbers.

Highlight a door's detail.
Paint the edges of the paneling in contrasting colors. Use painter's tape to guide your lines for a crisp, clean result.

Mix your planter shapes.
There's no need to make them match — the same goes for the plants. Try different sizes on either side of the door.

Put up a message board.
Grab some chalk to write a welcome message for special guests or leave a note for a delivery person.

Hang a bouquet or a wreath.
Put a flat-backed vessel on a wreath hook to hold real (or faux) stems and branches. Wrap snipped ends with a damp cloth so they'll stay hydrated. See pages 200–201 for easy wreaths.

Replace your gutters.
They protect your home from water damage and frame the roof. Newer models tend to be stronger, sturdier, scratch-resistant and clog-proof.

Deep-clean your exterior.
Pressure or power washing gets rid of built-up dirt, grime and mold. It's a slightly more advanced DIY project, so if you are hesitant, call the pros.

LAB TIP Don't underestimate the power of the welcome mat! It can be the perfect greeting, reflect a lighthearted personality, add a dash of color or make a natural focal point. Shake out your doormat every week to keep it doing its job.

CREATE an OUTDOOR LIVING SPACE

Breathe new life into your backyard, and it might become your favorite "room."

Stain your fence.

Think of your fence as the backdrop to your backyard: It's not the star of the show, but everything looks a little better when it's in tip-top shape. Give it a face-lift with a fresh coat of all-weather-proof stain.

Add an outdoor firepit.

Create an (almost) all-season backyard by adding a firepit for s'more-filled summer nights and cozy fall evenings. See page 163 for incredibly delish s'mores recipes.

Try hardscaping.

Your backyard doesn't have to be one big expanse of grass. For something different, add hard-scaping — it could be stone, pavers, bricks, wood or even gravel — to create a new terrace or outdoor area.

Design an outdoor lounge.

Start with an over-size outdoor sofa, then add pillows, blankets and a bar cart stocked with essentials. A large ottoman can double as a low table. Keep the same color scheme between indoors and out if you want to visually connect the spaces.

Vary the lighting.

Have a few spot-lights to illuminate areas like the garage or backyard, and add dedicated "task" lighting near each entry in the form of wall sconces or a porch ceiling light. Use accent lighting to highlight archi-tectural features and create ambience. For a magical ambience, string lights through the trees, around a garden or over a porch. Mix hanging LEDs or paper lan-terns with tabletop candles.

Plant a colorful, fragrant and/or edible garden.

See page 151 for advice about getting a container garden started.

Lay down a rug.

Anchor your patio's dining table with a patterned outdoor rug to add a touch of formality (and a comfy resting spot for bare feet).

Circle your chairs.

Organize chaises, lawn chairs and cushions to encour-age conversations that last late into the night.

LAB TIP Repel dirt by coating aluminum and wrought-iron furniture with car wax.

LAB TIP Many flagpoles that attach to houses aren't long enough to allow for flying a flag at half-staff. Instead, you can attach a mourning streamer or bow to the top of the flag (immediately beneath the ball or spearhead at the top of the pole).

FLY a FLAG PROPERLY

Follow the official U.S. Flag Code when flying Old Glory at home.

1 No flag pole? Hang the flag vertical.
The stars should be on the observer's left.

2 Avoid letting the flag touch the ground.
Fly your flag at half-staff (half-*mast* at sea) on these occasions: when the nation is in mourning, such as for the death of a government official; for remembrance; and from sunrise to noon on Memorial Day. When flying the flag at half-staff, first hoist it to the peak and then lower to the halfway position. To take the flag down, bring it to the top of the pole before lowering.

3 Illuminate your flag at night.
Custom dictates that you should display flags only from sunrise to sunset, unless they are properly lit during the hours of darkness.

4 Fly the American flag above other flags, including state and city flags.
If they all have to be at the same level (i.e., you're hanging them vertically), put the American flag on the left. Always hoist the American flag first and lower it last.

5 Check your flag's condition.
Flags that are overly worn, torn or faded should be properly disposed of. Contact your local American Legion post to find out if they have flag disposal ceremonies.

FOLD AN AMERICAN FLAG

1. Fold the lower, striped section of the flag over the blue field.

2. Fold over the folded bottom edge to meet the top edge.

3. Begin a triangular fold by bringing the striped corner of the folded edge to the top edge.

4. Turn the outer point inward, parallel with the top edge, to form a second triangle.

5. Continue until only the Union (the blue portion with white stars) is showing and the open edges are folded in.

TAKE CARE of YOUR YARD

By clearing, cutting and caring for your yard, the grass will never again seem greener on the other side.

Treat trouble spots.
Sprinkle soil over the area with a combination of grass seed and fertilizer. Keep dirt moist until the seeds sprout.

Get the right mower.
A walk-behind unit is best for less than 10,000 square feet of grass (just shy of a quarter acre). Anything larger, and you'll want a ride-on. Dull blades can cause sprouts to die, so make sure to have the machine serviced as needed.

Cure brittle brown grass.
It's easy for your lawn to dry out in the heat. Test soil in a few spots by pushing a screwdriver into the earth. If it doesn't go in smoothly to a depth of 6 inches, haul out the hose. Next, adjust your mowing height to 3½ inches. Taller grass helps reduce moisture loss from the soil and is better at standing up to hot weather.

Mow less.
If you keep grass blades longer in summer (read: mow the yard less often), it reduces the amount of watering you have to do — the shorter the grass, the more nourishment it needs. Also, leave trimmings on the lawn. While this temporarily looks a tad messy, it's healthier for the yard in the long term, as nutrients break down and reenter the soil.

Let leaves lie.
Fallen foliage is a necessary part of the ecosystem. As the leaves decompose, they help fertilize the soil. If you must get rid of leaves, compost them or use them for mulch in planting beds.

Clip away any dead branches.
Cut back branches that are encroaching on walkways or high-traffic areas to allow more sunlight and air to reach the center of trees and shrubs.

PRUNE LIKE A PRO

Cutting back overgrown flowering shrubs or fruit trees near your house will help plants produce more flowers and fruit, and help prevent diseases and pest infestations.

Ornamental grasses: Tie the tops of the grasses for quick and easy cutting, and then snip as close to the ground as possible. You can prune either in late fall or spring, depending on personal preference.

Semiwoody perennials: Cut back plantings like butterfly bushes and Russian sage to about 4 inches tall in late fall and get rid of dead leaves in the following spring.

Broad-leaved evergreens: Prune any injured foliage from evergreens like boxwood or holly or firethorn. Wait until early summer to hedge.

Flowering trees: Before roses and hydrangeas fully bloom, remove dead, damaged or crowded stems, and shape or cut back as desired.

WATER YOUR LAWN

Proper watering is crucial for maintaining a lush green lawn. Follow our tips to grow a resilient, healthy lawn.

1 Water in the morning.

Cooler temperatures and calm breezes help keep evaporation to a minimum. It also keeps the turf cooler during the hottest parts of the day, which means less stress on the grass. If it's not convenient to water in the morning, late afternoon is the next best time. Waiting to water until too late in the evening keeps lawns wet overnight, which can make the grass susceptible to diseases like fungus.

2 Soak 6 inches into the soil.

Conduct the screwdriver test: After watering the lawn, take a long-blade screwdriver and shove it straight down into the ground. The blade should easily penetrate the soil to a depth of 6 inches. If it doesn't, you're not watering enough.

3 Use pulsating sprinklers.

These sprinklers shoot out water horizontally at high velocity, so water is not as vulnerable to wind and evaporation as oscillating types, which spray the water straight up, and then rotate side to side.

4 Go easy with new grass.

Oscillating sprinklers are a gentler choice for new lawns until the grass takes root.

For newly planted grass seed, keep the top inch of the soil moist, but not soggy. Monitor and water regularly until the grass is 3 inches high, then water on your regular cycle. When mowing, take wide, slow turns to prevent the mower's wheels from tearing up the new lawn.

5 Look for signs of under- or over-watering.

Experts recommend watering clay soils once a week and sandy soils about every three days. Signs of underwatering include brittle, dry or brown grass. Signs of overwatering include mushrooms, weeds, spongy grass and runoff.

6 Get a timer.

You will never need to worry about having to shut off your sprinkler or wonder whether your lawn got enough water.

7 Be consistent.

Toggling between letting your lawn go dormant and keeping it watered is hard on the grass. It's far better to make a choice. Letting it go dormant like it does in the winter won't harm the grass as long as there's not a drought lasting longer than a month. A dormant lawn will come back to life after a good rainstorm.

LAB TIP Lawns in new housing developments often have compacted soil so hard that water can't sink in. If this is the case, water for 30 minutes, let the water soak in and repeat to avoid runoff.

PLANT a CONTAINER GARDEN

Container gardening is ideal for those with little or no outdoor space, or for adding versatility to gardens large and small. Containers offer unlimited possibilities of combinations — herbs, flowering annuals and perennials, bushes and shrubs, and even small trees like dwarf evergreens or lilacs.

What to Combine

One easy guideline for choosing the plants to combine in a single container is to include "a thriller, a spiller and a filler." That translates to at least one focal-point plant (the thriller), such as coleus or a geranium with multicolored leaves, with several plants that spill over the edge of the pot — such as petunias, Bacopa, creeping zinnias or ornamental sweet potatoes. Finally, add the fillers, which are plants with smaller leaves and flowers that add color and fill in the arrangement all season long. Good fillers include salvias, verbenas, ornamental peppers and wax begonias, as well as foliage plants like parsley or licorice plants. You may also want to include a plant for height, such as purple fountain grass, or a trellis or pillar with a vine. All told, you'll need five or six plants for an 18- or 24-inch container.

Container Sizes

It's easier to grow plants in large containers than small ones. That's because large containers hold more soil, which stays moist longer and resists rapid temperature fluctuations. Small hanging baskets are especially prone to drying out, and during hot summer weather you may need to water them twice a day to keep the plants alive.

Several factors help determine the size and depth of the container — the size and shape of a plant's root system; whether it is a perennial, annual or shrub; and how rapidly it grows. Root-bound plants, which have filled up every square inch of the soil available, dry out rapidly and won't grow well. Choose a large pot or tub for a mixed planting, one that will offer enough root space for all the plants you want to grow. Light-colored containers keep the soil cooler than dark containers.

The maximum size (and weight) of a container is limited by how much room you have, what will support it and whether you plan to move it. If your container garden is located on a balcony or deck, be sure to factor in the weight of furniture and people. How much weight your balcony or deck can safely hold depends on a variety

(continued on page 152)

LAB TIP Add a theme to your container gardens. Plant a salad garden with colorful lettuces, dwarf tomatoes, chives and parsley, or a pizza garden full of basil, tomatoes and peppers.

151

LAB TIP Mix and match textures and heights when planning your container gardens.

of factors, among them construction materials and age. If you're concerned, select lightweight pots and hire a structural engineer to run precise calculations.

Container Drainage

Whatever container you choose, drainage holes are essential. Without drainage, soil will become waterlogged and plants may die. Holes need not be large, just big enough that excess water can drain out. Self-watering and double-walled containers, hanging baskets and window boxes are useful for dealing with smaller plants that need frequent watering.

Container Preparation

Since containers are heavy once they're filled with soil, decide where they will be located and move them into position before filling and planting. If keeping them watered during the day is a problem, look for sites that get morning sun but are shaded during the hottest part of the day. Afternoon shade will reduce the amount of moisture plants need.

While your containers must have drainage holes, it's not necessary to cover the holes with pot shards or gravel before you add potting mix. The covering won't improve drainage, and pot shards may actually block the holes. Instead, prevent soil from washing out by placing a layer of paper towel or newspaper over the holes before adding potting mix. If your container is very deep, you can put a layer of gravel in the bottom to reduce the

(continued on page 154)

LAB TIP When temperatures start dropping, you may wish to bring your plants indoors. Ease your plants into the new environment by bringing them indoors for a few hours at a time (make sure to check for bugs beforehand). After two weeks or so, they should be ready to stay indoors for the season.

LAB TIP **Plants in small containers offer an opportunity to highlight interesting pottery.**

Selecting Plants for Containers

Almost any vegetable, flower, herb, shrub or small tree can grow successfully in a container. Dwarf and compact cultivars are best, especially for smaller pots. Select plants to suit the climate and the amount of sun or shade the container will receive. If you are growing fragrant plants, such as heliotrope (*Heliotropium arborescens*), place containers in a site protected from breezes, which will disperse the perfume.

Use your imagination and combine upright and trailing plants, edibles and flowers for pleasing and colorful effects. Container gardening can be enjoyed for one season and discarded, or designed to last for years. When designing permanent containers, remember that the plants will be less hardy than usual because their roots are more exposed to fluctuating air temperature. Nonhardy plants will need to have winter protection or be moved to a sheltered space. So consider how heavy the container will be and decide how you will move it before choosing a nonhardy plant.

amount of potting soil required.

Plain garden soil is too dense for container gardening. For containers up to 1 gallon in size, use a houseplant soil mixture. For larger containers, use a relatively coarse soilless planting mixture to maintain the needed water-and-air balance.

Premoisten soil either by watering it before you fill containers or by flooding the containers with water several times and stirring. Be sure the soil

is uniformly moist before planting.

If you are planting a mixed container, ignore spacing requirements and plant densely; you will need to prune the plants once they fill in. For trees and shrubs, trim off any circling roots and cover the root ball to the same level as it was set at the nursery. Firm the planter mixture gently and settle by watering thoroughly. Don't fill pots to the top with soil mixture — leave space for watering.

Container Gardening Care

Water container plants thoroughly. How often depends on many factors such as the weather and the size of the plants and pots. Don't let soil in containers dry out completely, as it's hard to rewet. A layer of mulch will help retain moisture. Keep mulch an inch or so away from plant stems — mulch that's too close can suffocate the plant, cause disease and/or provide a warm, welcoming environment for pests.

Container plants also benefit from regular feeding and fertilizing. Fertilizer enriches plant soil, encourages growth and health, and comes in a variety of types. Too much fertilizer can kill your plants, so carefully follow the instructions and pay attention to how your plants respond.

Remove tattered leaves and deadhead spent flowers. Prune back plants that get leggy or stop blooming. To keep mixed pots attractive, dig out or cut back any plants that don't grow well or that clash. You can add others or let existing plants in the container fill the space. Keep an eye out for pests like aphids and mites.

How to Propagate Succulents

You can clone succulents by splicing off clippings or removing leaves and encouraging them to sow their own roots.

1. Cut the heads. Use a sharp pair of scissors to snip a leaf-covered section of one of the stems that's at least 3 inches long. This is your cutting.

2. Pluck leaves. Succulents will propagate from individual leaves too. You can either pluck leaves from your clippings or from the parent plant. Hold the fleshy leaf close to the stem. Twist gently to remove cleanly. Small new roots and leaves will ultimately start to emerge from the leaf's base.

3. Arrange and water. Place your clippings and leaves, cut ends up, on a dish filled with fast-draining soil facing indirect sunlight. Leave for about three days or until the ends callus over. Once that happens, use a spray bottle to moisten—but not soak—the soil. Repeat whenever the soil is dry, roughly every four to five days. In about three to four weeks, tiny pink roots will start to sprout from your clippings.

4. Tend to the pups. After six or seven weeks, you'll notice baby pups (i.e., tiny leaves, the cutest things you've ever seen) emerging from the parent leaves. The parents may look shriveled. This is because they are feeding the pups with their own water and nutrients. Transfer your cuttings and leaves to containers of their own. Cover the new roots with $1/2$ inch of soil, sit back, and watch your garden grow.

GROW PRETTY PERENNIALS

These plants pop up every blooming season with fresh buds, refreshed colors and bold aromas—without you having to plant them each year. We've rounded up our favorites complete with zone requirements, sunlight needs and optimal blooming times.

Allium

These purple pom-pom flowers can be left untouched for years, especially since pests tend to avoid them. Their skinny stems rise to 30 inches, making them stand out against low-growers. *Zones 3–9; prefers full sun; blooms summer to fall*

Asters (*Astereae*)

With star-shaped flowers, asters can grow anywhere from 8 inches to 8 feet in height and are loved by pollinators. They really come to life in late summer. *Zones 3–8; prefers full sun; blooms late summer to fall*

Butterfly Bush

The lavender-pink blossoms on these shrubs attract tons of butterflies. The shrub requires annual pruning in the late winter or early spring to keep it in tip-top shape for the coming year. *Zones 5–10; prefers full sun; blooms summer to fall*

Coneflowers (*Echinacea*)

Make a bold statement by planting masses of coneflowers in pinks, purples, oranges and yellows. These trouble-free blooms grow fast, self-sow seeds all season long, attract butterflies and tolerate little or no water. *Zones 3–9; prefers full sun; blooms summer to fall*

Coral Bells (*Heuchera*)

The small bell-shaped flowers that spring up from this foliage plant attract hummingbirds. They're frequently used as groundcover, or as borders in woodlands or rock gardens. *Zones 4–8; prefers full sun or partial shade; blooms spring to summer*

Daylily (*Hemerocallis*)

Called the "perfect perennial," daylilies survive through almost anything. They come in a variety of colors and sizes. While each stem grows several flowers, the buds only bloom for one day. *Zones 4–9; prefers full sun or partial shade; blooms early summer*

Hostas

This low-maintenance foliage comes in a variety of green shades with white or purple flowers during summer or fall. Hostas do well in shade, but the lighter the leaves, the more sun they need to thrive. *Zones 3–9; prefers partial shade; blooms summer to fall*

Hydrangeas

Their large flower heads add dramatic touches of pink, lavender, blue and white to gardens. To ensure that they live a full life (50 years!), plant them in spring after the last spring frost or in fall before the first fall frost. *Zones 3–9; prefers partial sun; blooms summer to fall*

Lavender

This aromatic plant grows especially well in areas with hot temperatures and little rain. Another plus: Lavender naturally repels mosquitoes; see page 159 for more information. *Zones 5–9; prefers full sun; blooms late spring to early summer*

Phlox

Starting in early spring, low-growing phlox blooms as groundcover. During summer months, the tall variety — up to 5 feet in height — creates a colorful backdrop. The star-shaped flowers emit a strong fragrance and require little TLC. *Zones 2–9; prefers full sun but tolerates shade; blooms spring to summer*

Sage (*Salvias*)

This flowering kitchen herb works well as a garden border, attracting bees, hummingbirds and butterflies. Over time, they'll grow anywhere from 18 inches to 5 feet tall, despite heat or drought conditions. *Zones 5–10; prefers full sun; blooms spring to fall*

Shasta Daisy (*Leucanthemum*)

These short-lived perennials grow in clumps, filling up any empty spots with bright bursts of white and yellow. Bonus: You can cut the flowers at the stem for an instant vase filler or centerpiece (see page 210 for tips on transforming your table), and they'll regrow in no time. *Zones 5–8; prefers full sun; blooms late spring to fall*

Yarrow (*Achillea*)

This hardy and versatile perennial is as carefree as it gets — pest-resistant, quick to spread and a major pollinator attractant. Cut the red, yellow, pink or white flowers when their color starts to fade to encourage more growth. *Zones 3–9; prefers full sun; blooms summer*

LAB TIP Know your zone. As a general guide, check the USDA's Hardiness Zones, which can help you figure out which plants will flourish in your specific micro-conditions. Does your garden get full sun all day, or is it mostly shady? A plant's tag has notes about what kind of light it needs and when it should be planted.

MAKE YOUR OWN NONTOXIC WEED KILLER

Common household supplies like salt and newspaper can kill weeds pretty much instantly, leaving your garden to sprout in all its glory.

Landscape Fabric
Generally made from synthetic fibers, landscape fabric acts as a physical barrier to stop unwanted plants from sprouting up. Top it with a layer of mulch or straw.

Trowel
A trowel and a little elbow grease can conquer invaders. Try to pull from beneath the soil so that you can get the root out. Waiting until after a rainstorm (when the ground is softer) can also help.

Newspaper
Cover low-growing weeds with newspaper; eventually the lack of sunlight will exterminate them. Weigh the newspaper down with grass clippings, wood chips, shredded bark or mulch.

Mulch
Mulch is a catchall name for material, such as dead leaves or compost, that covers your soil, keeping it cool and wet, and eliminates the light that weeds need to grow. Keep it around 2 inches deep. Avoid putting it on your lawn, since it will kill your grass.

Boiling Water
Boil tap water, add a pinch of salt, and pour the hot, salty water into cracks in your driveway or sidewalk.

Other Plants
Plant groundcovers, flowers and garden crops that will naturally beat out weeds.

Edging
Physical barriers like lawn edgings and retaining walls are a long-lasting solution for keeping weeds at bay.

Repel Mosquitoes

They may be great food for birds and bats, but you definitely don't want mosquitoes hanging around your backyard. Fortunately, natural repellants can get rid of them.

Dry things out.
Make your outdoor living areas less hospitable to mosquito eggs by removing any standing water (including the water in clogged rain gutters, birdbaths and flowerpots). Cut back any high grass or brush that creates shady or damp spots that mosquitoes favor.

Use the power of scent.
Some strong smells hide the scent of people (something that attracts mosquitoes) and prevent the insects from wanting to get close enough to bite you. Several plants do double duty by producing scents that please humans and disgust mosquitoes. The aroma needs to be in the air around you, at the very least, but ideally on your skin.

To get the maximum effect of these natural mosquito-repellent plants, consider planting them in your garden. Crush herb leaves in your hands to release their perfume and essential oils, and then rub the leaves and their oils on your skin.

SCENTS THAT MOSQUITOES AVOID

Basil

Lemon Balm

Catnip

Peppermint

Rosemary

Citrosa Geranium, or "Mosquito Plant"

Lavender

Sage

LAB TIP Some of these plants may cause skin irritation. Always do a patch test on a small section of your skin before using — and skip using altogether if you have dry or sensitive skin, or if you're allergic to any of these plants.

START YOUR OWN COMPOST BIN

Composting — creating natural fertilizer from decayed plant matter — is good for your plants. It's good for the earth, too: keeping food scraps and yard waste out of landfills reduces emissions.

1 Choose the right space.
If you're setting up outside, choose a bin that's about 3 feet in diameter and not much higher than your waist. A lid will help if you're worried about the way the compost pile will look or smell. You can also set up a mini station in your kitchen.

2 Take note of what you can (and can't) compost.
Much kitchen and garden refuse can go into the bin, including eggshells, cut flowers, coffee grounds (and paper filters), tea and tea bags, fruit and vegetable scraps, and even hair. Dairy and animal products will cause compost to smell and attract pests, so toss those in the regular household garbage. The same goes for fats, oils and pet waste.

3 Keep it balanced.
Green waste — like produce and grass clippings — supplies the compost with nitrogen, key for healthy soil. Brown waste — like dry leaves or paper bags — is rich in carbon, which helps break down the other scraps. Aim for four parts brown to one part green (in volume) for the ideal balance.

4 Give your pile some TLC.
Every few weeks, check that your compost is getting the air and water it needs to thrive. If it seems dry, add a sprinkling of water, then mix. If you're not seeing progress, add green material and make sure to keep the pile moist. If it's smelly and wet, add brown material and turn it more often. It also helps to have earthworms in the bin. Different items break down at different rates, but you should start to see results after about a month or two.

5 Use it.
Your compost is ready when it looks and smells like soil. Incorporate it into, or sprinkle it onto, your garden beds. Treat it as a natural fertilizer to nurture soil (not replace it), and add it a couple of times a year for best results.

LAB TIP Whether you're in an apartment or a house without a backyard, you can set up a mini collection station right in your kitchen so you don't have to trash food scraps. Get a compost bin with a tight-fitting lid, line it with a biodegradable bag and store full bags in your freezer until you can go drop them off at the compost site or have them picked up.

THROW the BEST BBQS

How do you spell "summer"? We spell it B-B-Q.
Here's how to put on a super-fun one.

Day Before

1 **Prep as much in advance as possible.** Peel, chop, make the marinades.

2 **Grill vegetables that can be served cold** or at room temperature, such as squash, eggplant, plum tomatoes, onions and fennel.

3 **Make some hearty salads** such as a kale or *panzanella* salad.

Day Of

1 **Set up a buffet.** Position your buffet under an overhang or umbrella to protect it from the elements. Then order its contents this way for easy cruising: plates, sides, buns, meats, fixings and flatware.

2 **Separate the food and drinks.** A separate beverage station lets guests mix drinks and mingle. Stock the bar with cups, straws (to double as stirrers) and plenty of ice — a large metal pail will keep bottles and cans frosty, but consider an insulated or lidded cooler for ice used in drinks. Label a trash can by the bar so revelers can recycle before they replenish.

3 **Stock amenities.** Help company stay comfortable outdoors all day — and into the night. Stick sunblock, bug spray, hand wipes and, if it might turn chilly, light blankets in big baskets around your yard.

4 **Raid your home office.** Stick-on arrow flags or Post-its make perfect drink labels. Guests can jot their names on tags, yet the flags pull off quickly post-fete. Rubber bands will secure napkin-wrapped cutlery sets so partygoers can grab utensils one-handed from the buffet. Safety-pin one or two old or unused keys to the underside of each corner of your tablecloth to keep it from blowing off.

GET YOUR GRILL READY

A clean grill will make your food taste so much better. Get your grill ready with this three-step guide.

1 Remove and clean the grates.

Wipe or brush off as much of the big, loose debris as you can with a mesh or nylon scrub pad or a brush. In a sink or large bucket, mix up a sudsy solution of a grease-cutting dish liquid and hot water, and place the grates in to soak. If they don't completely fit in, immerse one half, soak, then flip it over to get the other side. After soaking 15 to 30 minutes, scrub the grates clean with a sturdy grill brush or scrubbing pad. Take extra care with porcelain grates, because you don't want to scrub too hard, nick, drop or otherwise damage them.

2 Clean the inside.

With the grates removed, brush down the inside to clear out any loose particles that have collected in the bottom and around the sides of the grill. Scrape off any large peeling flakes of carbon and grease, and if yours is a charcoal grill, empty the ash catcher. Don't forget to clean the drip pan and grease cup in warm soapy water, and line them with aluminum foil so they'll be easier to clean next time.

3 Clean the exterior.

Mix up another bath of warm sudsy dish liquid and water and wipe down the exterior, handle, side trays and any bottom doors with a sponge or cloth, or use a grease-cutting all-purpose cleaner.

TAKE YOUR S'MORES TO THE NEXT LEVEL

While the three basic ingredients of s'mores — chocolate, graham cracker and marshmallow — are perfect on their own, they leave room for endless improvisation.

- Swap the chocolate for a miniature candy bar or peanut butter cup.

- Smear a gob of salted caramel on the graham crackers.

- Replace the chocolate with a very ripe blueberry, strawberry or blackberry. It's like pie!

- Toast the marshmallow like normal, then sandwich it between two chocolate-chip cookies instead of chocolate and graham crackers.

- Roll the toasted marshmallow in coconut.

GRILL ANYTHING

You too can be a grill master. Juicy burgers and hot dogs may get top billing, but tons of other meats, seafood, fruits and vegetables benefit from a little time over an open flame.

	Baby Back Ribs	Burger	Chicken (bone-in)	Chicken Breasts (boneless, skinless)
PROTIEN				
PREP	Make your own BBQ sauce: In a saucepan, combine $1/2$ tsp. salt, 2 cups ketchup, 1 cup apple cider, 2 Tbsp. Worcestershire sauce, 2 Tbsp. molasses, 2 Tbsp. cider vinegar, 2 Tbsp. brown sugar, 2 Tbsp. yellow mustard, $1/2$ tsp. ground black pepper, and $1/4$ tsp. cayenne; heat to boiling over high heat. Reduce heat and simmer, uncovered, 30 to 40 min. or until sauce thickens slightly, stirring occasionally. Makes about $2^{1}/_2$ cups.	Use your thumb to make a shallow $1^{1}/_2$-inch-wide indent in the top of each patty. This will help the patties stay flat, so you'll end up with burgers, not baseballs. Be sure to grill them indent side up first.	Consider brining your chicken to lock in moisture. For every 3 lbs of chicken, take 5 cups of tepid water and whisk in two big palmfuls of salt and a big palmful of sugar until dissolved. Before adding the chicken parts, take a small sip of the brine. It should taste almost unpalatably salty. Add chicken, then brine in the fridge for 4 to 6 hr. Pat chicken dry before putting it on the grill.	Marinate the meat in the refrigerator. If using a marinade as a basting or dipping sauce, set aside a portion for later before adding it to the raw food. Wash basting brushes with hot soapy water after using them, and discard leftover marinade that came in contact with raw chicken.
HEAT	Indirect (covered), medium-high, then direct (uncovered)	Direct (uncovered), medium-high	Indirect (covered), medium-low, turning occasionally	Direct (uncovered), medium
TIME	Cook with indirect heat for 30 to 35 min. (Use the upper rack of the grill if you have one), followed by direct (uncovered) for 4 to 6 min. per side.	Cook 4 to 5 min. per side for medium. Don't press down on the patties while they cook or you'll squeeze out some of the tasty juices.	Cook for 35 to 45 min. (wings will take less time), and start grilling with the bone side down.	Cook 5 to 8 min. per side (165°F internal temperature).

LAB TIP Marinades and basting sauces, many of which have a high sugar content, will burn if the grill temperature is too hot or if exposed to heat for too long. A hot grill is normally not a problem with quick-cooking cuts (such as skinless, boneless breasts); longer-cooking cuts (such as bone-in chicken parts) should be cooked over lower heat. And don't start basting until the chicken is almost fully cooked.

	Flank Steak (3/4 to 1 inch thick)	Salmon Fillet	Shrimp	Hot Dogs
PROTIEN				
PREP	Try rubbing meat with spices, or toss it with a mixture of soy sauce, grated garlic and ginger. Refrigerate for up to 8 hr. before grilling for maximum flavor.	Try this sweet-and-spicy rub: Combine 3 Tbsp. brown sugar, 2 tsp. paprika, 1 tsp. garlic powder, 1 tsp. onion powder, and ½ tsp. black pepper and set aside. Pat salmon fillets dry. Brush fillets all over with oil, and sprinkle with salt. Coat flesh sides with BBQ rub. Push soaked skewers through salmon lengthwise; place them, skin side down, on grill.	Look for large, already-peeled and deveined ones that won't fall through the grates. You could also thread onto skewers.	Prevent dogs from falling through the grill grates by lining them up perpendicular to the grates. Then use a long spatula to roll them all rather than turning each one individually.
HEAT	Direct (uncovered), medium-high	Direct (uncovered), medium-high	Direct (uncovered), medium-high	Direct (uncovered), medium-high
TIME	Cook for 4 to 6 min. per side for medium rare.	Cook 3 to 5 min. per side.	Grill until opaque throughout and uniformly pink, 2 to 3 min. per side.	Cook 6 to 8 min., turning occasionally.

Grill Fruits and Vegetables

So many fruits take well to the grill — they become juicier, without getting that "stewed" flavor, and the sugars brown and caramelize. Use direct (uncovered) heat, at medium-high temperatures, for fruits and vegetables.

FRUIT OR VEG	PREP	TIME
Asparagus	Line up perpendicular to the grates.	4 to 6 min., turning occasionally
Avocado	Halve and remove pit, and leave skin on. Brush lightly with olive oil.	1 to 3 min., cut side down until charred
Citrus	Halve or cut into wedges.	1 to 3 min., cut side down until charred
Corn	Shuck the corn and rub with olive oil.	3 to 5 min., turning occasionally, until charred
Mushrooms	Slice lengthwise, or thread whole onto a skewer.	5 to 10 min. (gill side up)
Onions	Slice onions into rounds, brush with olive oil and season with salt and pepper.	5 to 6 min.
Peppers	Quarter peppers lengthwise and discard seeds. Toss with olive oil, salt and pepper.	3 to 4 min. per side
Pineapple	Remove rind and cut into 1/4-inch-thick triangles or rounds.	2 to 5 min. per side
Plum Tomatoes	Halve tomatoes lengthwise.	2 to 3 min. per side, grilling cut side first
Romaine	Halve romaine lengthwise and brush with a tiny bit of olive oil.	2 to 3 min., turning occasionally, until charred and just beginning to wilt
Watermelon	Cut the watermelon into 1/2-inch-thick triangles, and cut off the rinds. Brush lightly with olive oil.	1 to 2 min. per side

SUPPLIES
- Cutting board
- Ice cream scoop
- Small knife/ apple corer
- Spigot
- Watermelon

Enjoy

MAKE a WATERMELON KEG

Fun and fruity, a watermelon keg is a delightful way to serve punch at your next outdoor shindig.

1 Prep the watermelon.

Wash the watermelon of any dirt or grocery store gunk. Cut about a third of an inch off each watermelon end. One flat end will become the base, holding the watermelon upright, and the other will be the opening at the top.

2 Start scooping and scraping.

With an ice cream scoop, remove the middle of the watermelon from the top side and pour out excess watermelon juice. This makes scooping easier and keeps your hands from swimming in liquid. Set the fruit aside for snacking, garnishing or grilling (see page 167). Leave about 2 inches of fruit at the bottom of the melon so the keg won't leak.

After removing the guts of the watermelon, scrape the inside walls of any remaining pink to make more room for your drink.

3 Attach the spigot.

Once you've hollowed out the inside, find the best-looking side of the watermelon and face it forward. This is the spot you want to place your spigot. Drill a small hole 2 to 3 inches above the bottom of the watermelon with an apple corer or a small knife. Insert the spigot. Be sure it fits tight and secure. (Try fastening a nut to the spigot on the inside of the watermelon to ensure it stays in place.)

4 Fill it up.

Pour in your favorite concoction (party punch, homemade juice, margaritas, sangria, watermelon water, etc.) and serve. For ease and prettiness, try propping it on a cake stand. Otherwise, be sure it's standing upright and solid on the table. The watermelon keg lasts about 6 hours without leaking, so keep refilling as much as you want. Post-event, toss the shell into your composting bin (see page 161 for composting info) and hold on to the spigot for your next keg.

FILL YOUR KEG WITH AN EASY SUMMER PUNCH

Gather raspberries, lemons and ginger ale. Strain the watermelon juice you set aside while carving the keg. Next, muddle a handful of raspberries and mix them into the juice. Add this mixture to the keg. Pour in the ginger ale, then finish with four thick slices of lemon and another handful of raspberries. You can spike the punch by tossing in a few jiggers of vodka, tequila or rum, but aim to be conservative. It's always easier to add more alcohol.

PACK the PERFECT COOLER

Keep your food cool, safe and ready
for noshing and nom-nomming.

Layer with logic.
In general, what's on top should be what you'll eat first. Put perishables on the bottom (especially if meat is raw and juices could leak) so they won't be exposed to hot air when someone grabs a soda. Or use a separate cooler for drinks.

Chill out.
Blocks of ice stay frozen longer than cubes. Buy gel packs, or fill quart-size milk cartons with water and freeze for DIY chilling (about 1 carton per 4 quarts of cooler capacity). Layer ice on top of food once packed — cold travels downward.

Plan ahead.
Bring foods and snacks that get better after sitting around, like grain salads, hearty sandwiches (such as muffuletta), antipasti and dips.

Freeze what you can.
Put sandwiches, fruit like grapes and mango, and juice boxes in the freezer overnight — they'll stay cool longer and help keep the rest of the contents cold.

Assemble the Ultimate Picnic Kit

Pack this ready-to-go kit in a lidded plastic bin or basket, and you'll be all set to eat anywhere, anytime.

- **Reusable Plates, Utensils, Cups and Napkins**
Going reusable means you'll have dishes to clean, but plates won't wilt under the weight of juicy food, and it's more economical in the long run (not to mention better for the planet).

- **Plastic Tablecloth or Old Shower Curtain**
Spread a waterproof covering on a park table or on the grass to prevent

a soggy seat. You can always cover the waterproof surface with your favorite picnic blanket for comfort and style.

- **Bug-Repellent Lantern**
In addition to providing a little ambiance when the sun gets low, these helpful lanterns also ward away uninvited guests. (See page 159 for more tips on keeping mosquitoes at bay.)

- **Long-Necked Utility Lighter**
Matches can get wet, but a long-necked lighter is perfect for lighting your lantern or getting a park grill going. (See pages 165–167 for tips on grilling anything and everything.)

- **Wet Wipes**
Keep a pack handy to clean hands, mop up spills, and wipe down dishes before you bring them home for a more thorough wash.

LAB TIP Pack individually portioned pasta salads in mason jars for the whole crew. In each jar, add layers of vinaigrette, drained and rinsed chickpeas, sliced cherry tomatoes, kalamata olives, cooked and cooled pasta, arugula, and feta. When it's time to eat, just mix and enjoy. The perfectly portable lidded jar is easy to eat out of and makes clean-up a breeze. Just don't forget the forks!

BONUS RECIPE

Homemade Potato Salad

Serves **6**
Total time: **30 minutes**

Place 2 lbs baby yellow potatoes in a medium pot and cover with cold water. Bring to a boil, add $1/2$ Tbsp. kosher salt, reduce heat and simmer until just tender, 12 to 15 min. Meanwhile, toss $1/2$ medium red onion, finely chopped, with 3 Tbsp. white wine vinegar and $1/2$ tsp. each salt and pepper and let sit, tossing occasionally. Run potatoes under cold water to cool. Drain well and pat dry, then halve any that are large. Whisk 3 Tbsp. olive oil and 1 tsp. Dijon mustard into vinegar mixture. Add potatoes and toss to coat. Fold in $1/2$ cup thawed frozen peas and $1/4$ cup fresh dill, roughly chopped.

ORGANIZE YOUR GARAGE and SHED

Instead of using these spaces as dumping grounds for anything and everything, reclaim prime storage real estate with these simple decluttering tips — you may even make room for the car!

Hang tools.
Rather than leaning lawn essentials against the wall, keep shovels, rakes, pruning shears and other garden tools within reach by mounting them on a pegboard panel. Once it's installed and painted, the storage possibilities are endless: Even big items like hoses and wheelbarrows can be roped up with strong bungee cords.

Repurpose home basics.
Creativity can give old kitchen organizers fresh life. A magnetic knife rack can be repurposed to hold items like wrenches, pliers and scissors. Old film canisters, mini mason jars and pillboxes can become new homes for nuts, bolts and nails: Label them and tuck them neatly away in long horizontal spice trays to tidy up your active workspace.

Opt for bins.
Limit rummaging by stowing similar items in labeled or clear bins. You'll make your life a little easier (and save your back) if you store bigger bins with heavier items in low, easily accessible places and smaller, lighter bins higher up. Extension cords, rags and other bulky items can live in wire baskets for visibility.

Use every inch of space.
Take advantage of vertical space. Tuck bikes and sports equipment below wall-mounted shelves, or suspend them from a garage ceiling so they won't hog square footage. Free up precious counter space by installing rails you can use to hang frequently used items in baskets, on hooks or inside tool holders.

LAB TIP Take your entertaining game to the next level by creating and perfecting your own signature cocktail or mocktail to serve.

CHAPTER 6

ENTERTAIN & CELEBRATE

PLAN the PERFECT PARTY

Professional caterers are expert party planners. Their smart suggestions work no matter what kind of event you're planning.

Set a crystal-clear time frame.
We've all been to the "cocktail party" that went through the night (without dinner). Be clear about the party's time frame to avoid misconstrued expectations.

Buy the right amount of food.
It's easy to overestimate the appetites of party guests. If you're planning a multicourse meal, go light on the apps. Caterers advise a big handful — about 1 cup — of salad, with 2 Tbsp. of dressing per person. For pasta, aim for 2 to 4 oz of dried pasta, $4\frac{1}{2}$ oz of fresh and 7 oz of filled pasta (like ravioli) per person. If you're serving appetizer bites, plan for 8 to 10 hors d'oeuvres per person. As for side dishes, consider $\frac{1}{4}$ to $\frac{1}{2}$ lb per guest.

Greet guests with an on-theme cocktail.
Think mimosas for brunch or champagne served in a coupe for an engagement celebration.

Let your appetizers do the decorating.
For cocktail parties, hors d'oeuvres are the focus — so make them look super-amazing. Hummus, flatbreads, tomato dishes, ratatouille, and pasta-and-vegetable salads are all bountiful and attractive options.

Serve food on the rocks.
Create your own chilled server by nestling a smaller bowl atop a larger bowl filled with crushed ice. For a special touch, try freezing flowers or herbs inside a few ice cubes you can display in the bowl.

Turn your kitchen into the buffet.
Free up space in your dining room and living room and ensure hot foods stay at the perfect temperature.

Plan for garbage.
Before the party starts, line your garbage can with a few bags. Then, when one is full, simply remove it and a fresh one will already be waiting.

STOCK a HOME BAR

Keep the following items on hand and you'll be able to handle any occasion or drink request.

Alcohol

- Blended whiskey
- Bourbon
- Brandy
- Champagne
- Craft beer (pilsner, IPA, porter and stout)
- Gin
- Liqueurs (coffee, orange and herbal)
- Rum
- Scotch
- Sherry (dry and sweet)
- Sour mash whiskey
- Tequila
- Vermouth (dry and sweet)
- Vodka
- Wine (red, white and sparkling)

Mixers

- Club soda
- Fruit juice (such as cranberry and orange)
- Soft drinks
- Sparkling and still waters (flavored and plain)
- Tomato or seasoned vegetable juice
- Tonic water

Barware
(6 to 8 of each)

- Coupes
- Short glasses
- Tall glasses
- Wineglasses

Garnishes and Flavorings

- Bitters, for champagne cocktails and old-fashioneds
- Citrus (lemon, lime and orange) whole, slices, wedges or peels
- Coarse salt, for margaritas
- Cocktail onions, for Gibsons
- Cream of coconut, for piña coladas
- Ice (preferably coarsely crushed)
- Maraschino cherries, for Manhattans
- Olives, for martinis
- Simple syrup, for sweet cocktails
- Tabasco sauce, for Bloody Marys
- Worcestershire sauce, for Bloody Marys

Equipment

- Blender
- Bottle opener
- Citrus squeezer
- Coasters
- Cocktail napkins
- Cocktail shaker or pitcher
- Corkscrew
- Cutting board
- Dishtowel
- Drink stirrers
- Ice bucket
- Jigger
- Paring knife, for fruit peels
- Strainer

LAB TIP
Rather than stocking separate glasses, pick one favorite and use it for both reds and whites.

LAB TIP Round up when party planning. Generally, one pound of ice per person, one bottle of wine for every two guests and two bottles of beer per person will keep drinks flowing for 2 to 3 hours. Your guests will likely sip 1½ drinks per person per hour. For children or a party without alcohol, count on three 8 oz glasses of juice or soda per guest.

BE the BEST BARTENDER

Cheers! Salud! Sláinte! Regardless of how you toast, here are a few tips and tricks for great drinks.

Chill cocktail and beer glasses ahead of time.

Freeze distilled water in silicone molds to get pure-tasting ice that won't leave a strange taste in your drink.

Handle glasses by the stem to avoid leaving finger marks and warming the contents.

Add carbonated beverages at the last minute, even to punches.

Avoid spills by filling glasses three-quarters full, not to the brim.

Keep a kitchen towel handy; making drinks can be messy.

Stir drinks mixed with ice. Gentle stirring causes the ice to melt, making for colder drinks, and helps enhance aroma and flavor.

Use a shaker to fully blend fruit juice and other ingredients.

WHIP UP SOME CLASSIC COCKTAILS

Impress your guests by keeping a few classic cocktail recipes up your sleeve. After all, there's nothing like sipping on a nice cocktail to make you feel just a little more sophisticated.

Martini

Makes **1**
Total time: **5 minutes**

Before starting, ensure that all your glassware and mixing glasses are chilled. Fill a mixing glass with ice and pour a splash of vermouth into the glass to coat the ice. Pour out the extra vermouth. Then mix 2½ oz gin with ½ oz vermouth. Stir 18 times, ideally with a proper cocktail stirring spoon. Strain into a chilled martini glass and garnish with a twist of grapefruit or lemon, or an olive.

Margarita

Makes **4**
Total time: **5 minutes**

In a medium pitcher, combine ¾ cup white tequila, ½ cup fresh lime juice and ½ cup Cointreau. If desired, rub rims of 4 glasses with a lime slice and dip in coarse salt and lime zest to coat. Add ice and pour drink on top. Serve with lime slices.

Old-Fashioned

Makes **1**
Total time: **5 minutes**

**Place 1 small sugar cube
into a rocks glass, top
with 3 dashes of bitters
and 1 teaspoon water,
and stir to nearly dis-
solve sugar and coat the
bottom of the glass.**

**Add a large ice cube to
the glass, then top with
2 oz bourbon and stir
until drink is cold, about
20 times.**

**Squeeze a 1-inch-wide
strip of orange peel over
the glass, then drop it in.**

KNOW YOUR WINE

Understanding a few key tasting concepts is all it takes to find new ways to enjoy wine. Impress your friends and enhance your knowledge by using the five S's of tasting wine.

1 See
Note the bottle, the country and the area, and then pour the wine. Observe the color, clarity and opacity of the wine. This is best done against a white surface.

2 Swirl
Either on the table or in your hand, swirl the glass in a circular motion. Are there long drips that run down the inside of the glass that stay awhile? These are "legs" and inform you of the wine's viscosity.

3 Sniff
Stick your nose into the glass and take a whiff. Evaluate the bouquet. You might smell fruit or flowers. You also might pick up on the wood from the barrel or other flavors. Close your eyes and have fun with it. Your vocabulary is your only limit!

4 Sip
Take a small mouthful, hold it in your mouth for 3 to 5 seconds, and let it rest so that your tongue is enveloped. With pursed lips, take in a little air and move the wine around. Oxygen will release more flavor.

5 Savor
Take in the wine. What is the mouthfeel? Heavy or light? Are you getting sweet, sour, bitter, fruity or mellow notes? Is there a pleasant balance or a bitter finish or aftertaste? Or is it gone in a matter of seconds? Most important, do you like it?

Keep Your Wine Fine

While gadgets are great, the good news is that you don't need to go all out to store your wine. A little thoughtful management is all it takes to prevent your vino from becoming vinegar.

Pay attention to temperatures. If you are storing wine for longer than a month, keep it between 53°F and 57°F. To serve a white, chill it to between 45°F and 52°F. Reds should be served only slightly chilled, from 58°F to 65°F (not room temperature).

Store opened bottles in the fridge. Wine is at its best within four to six hours of opening a bottle, but that doesn't mean you can't save it for another few days. To keep it at its best, both red and white should be left in the fridge — but remember to take the red out about half an hour before serving.

If you don't have a fridge or cooler, don't stock up. Buy what you'll drink over the course of a month. Stash bottles in a cool, dark spot, but never on top of the fridge — it's too warm.

Let your red breathe. Red wines are generally best when uncorked and allowed to "breathe" for about 15 minutes before serving.

PAIR WINE with FOOD

Tradition says that white wine goes with white meats, fish and seafood; red wine accompanies meats and richly sauced dishes; and blush and sparkling wines go with anything. Today, the rules are — thankfully — less strict. The best guide is your own taste.

Pair like with like.

In general, light wines, both white and red, best complement light and delicate foods. Bolder wines of both colors stand up to richer, more assertive foods.

There's a wine for every occasion.

You can even drink wine at a BBQ! A Riesling or Prosecco pairs well with hot dogs, while a Rioja or Beaujolais goes great with a burger.

> LAB TIP If you're serving only wine, offer a choice of red, white and perhaps even sparkling. If wine is part of a more complete bar setup, white wine is the most commonly requested, so stock up.

Elevate a simple cheese platter with the perfect wine.

Rieslings, especially those with high acidity and a touch of sweetness, are a good match for many cheeses. Champagne or other sparkling dry whites also get along well with most cheeses, and are good partners with runny, creamy Brie or other triple-creams. Try a Sauvignon Blanc bursting with grassy, crisp apple flavor with soft goat cheese, fresh or aged. If you prefer red wines, go for a big, fruity Australian Shiraz with a hard cheese like aged Cheddar or Gouda, or try some Spanish Manchego with a glass of Rioja. Strong blue cheeses do best with sweet wines that have some backbone—think Port or Sauternes.

Go beyond red and white.

Try a rosé in place of a white wine or an orange wine in place of a light, fruity red at summer gatherings. Rosé is made by crushing red wine grapes and immediately removing their skins. For orange wine, white grapes go through the red wine making process; white grapes are left in contact with their skins for anything from four days to a year. So while rosé is made with red grapes, it drinks more like a white—and while orange wine is made with white grapes, it has more tannins.

Remove the foil.

As you unravel the foil, hold the cork securely in case it pops on its own. Loosen the cage so it easily slips off the lip of the bottle.

Start twisting.

Hold the bottle tightly — using a cloth napkin or kitchen towel for firmer grip, if necessary — while aiming it away from your body and face. Gently twist the bottle (not the cork) until the cork loosens and easily pops out. It usually takes about six solid twists for the cork to pop.

Let the champagne sit for a second.

Give bubbles time to subside. Then pour bubbly into stemmed wineglasses (flute, tulip- or egg-shaped) to prevent people's hands from warming up the wine. Aim to fill each glass about two-thirds full.

UNCORK CHAMPAGNE

You know it's a special occasion when someone pops a bottle of bubbly. While a fizzy explosion looks awesome in the movies, it's not ideal in the middle of your living room. Steer clear of a messy — and scary — uncorking by following this foolproof guide.

Chill your bottle to about 45°F.

To prevent a foamy mess, chill champagne in the fridge for at least 3 hours before serving. Short on time? Wrap a bottle in wet paper towel layers and stick in the freezer for up to 30 minutes.

LAB TIP Restore the bubbles in flat champagne by dropping a raisin or two into the bottle.

CURE a HANGOVER

No one knows exactly what causes hangovers, but one hypothesis is that alcohol triggers the release of inflammatory chemicals into the body. Unfortunately, scientists have yet to discover an immediate, magical cure.

Eat a little something. Alcohol can affect your blood sugar levels, so getting a bite to eat can help get these levels back up to normal. Try some lean protein, complex carbohydrates and healthy fats, but steer clear of fried and sugary foods, which can worsen hangover symptoms.

Take ibuprofen, aspirin or naproxen for the headache. (Do not take acetaminophen within 24 hours of drinking alcohol, as this can cause liver damage.)

Get some (light) exercise, provided you're feeling up to it, and remember to hydrate throughout. Don't push yourself, however, since a hard workout has the potential to make you feel more exhausted.

Stay hydrated. As a diuretic, alcohol pulls water out of your system (i.e., it makes you urinate more often), which can lead to dehydration. Offset (and prevent) any alcohol-induced dehydration that may cause headaches or dizziness by sipping water. As a general rule, drink half your body weight (in ounces) over the course of the following day. So, if you weigh 160 pounds, you'd want to drink around 80 ounces of water, or 10 cups.

Replenish your electrolytes, the essential minerals that your body loses during a night of drinking. Watermelon, banana, strawberries, avocado, coconut water and 100% fruit juice are good choices.

Sleep and rest. Lack of sleep can exacerbate symptoms like fatigue, headache and dizziness.

Avoid the "hair of the dog." Drinking more alcohol to reduce the effects of a hangover can lead to an even worse hangover the next day, or the development of unhealthy drinking habits.

CREATE a CHEESE BOARD

Use this guide for amazing taste-and-texture snack combos, then experiment to find your faves!

Semi-Firm Cheeses	Fresh Cheeses	Firm Cheeses
Dark Bread	Wafer Crisps	Crackers
+	+	+
Manchego	Goat Cheese	Aged Gouda
+	+	+
Cranberries and Almonds	Sun-Dried Tomatoes	Dried Apricots

Soft Cheeses

Blue Cheeses

Baguette

Oatcakes

+

+

Brie

Blue Cheese

+

+

Pear
Slices

Walnuts and
Honey

SCAN ME!

HOW TO
SERVE
CHEESE

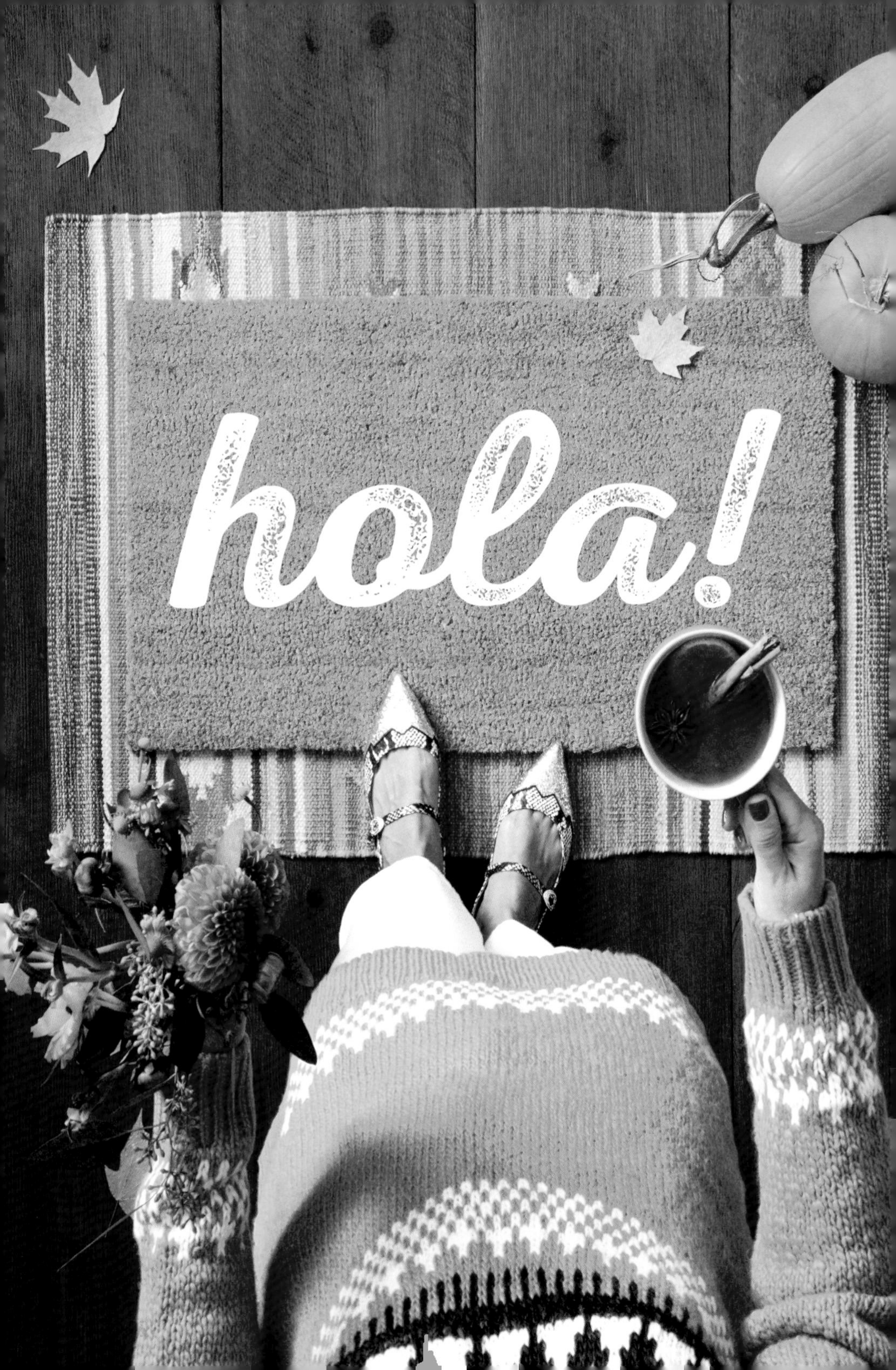
hola!

WELCOME HOUSEGUESTS

Our recommendations for making your house more welcoming for guests definitely do not involve shoving everything into a closet, then posting a sign that says "Do not open" — although, honestly, that could work in a pinch. For real speed-cleaning advice, see page 46.

Replace or clean the mat inside your front door. A dirty or worn mat won't trap dirt, leaving carpets and floors vulnerable to stains from tracked-in soil. If your mat isn't washable, shake it out, then vacuum both sides.

Clear some space. Visitors don't want to search for a spot to put down their glass. It's also a little nerve-racking for them to have to worry that they might accidentally bump a side table and break something. If you're a collector, invest in a display case where you could show your stuff off while protecting your items at the same time.

Manage your pets (and their stuff). Even if your pets are clean, seeing their beds, toys and litter box can make it seem as if your home isn't. Invest in, and use, a lint roller to pick up hair, and find a discreet spot for pet things.

Turn your thermostat down a notch. More people inside will make your house warmer.

Stock up on guests' favorite drinks, snacks and sweets to help them feel welcomed. Ask about and honor food allergies, and try to accommodate special diets.

Add extras like a hairdryer or a luggage rack to the guest room. Stash extra towels, toiletries and toilet paper. Clear out some space in the closet and a dresser for guests to unpack.

Place a vase of fresh flowers and a great book on the night-stand — it's a thoughtful way of saying, "I'm so glad you're here to visit!"

CARVE
the PERFECT
PUMPKIN

Follow our advice to
make the pumpkin of
your dreams.

1. **Choose a fresh pumpkin** with a sturdy stem, no bruises and a flat bottom so it won't roll while you carve.

2. **Turn the pumpkin on its side** and cut the lid from the bottom, not the top. (A lid lets you reach in and scoop out the insides.) Cutting from the bottom helps preserve the pumpkin's structure and prevents the sides from caving in later.

LAB TIP If you do carve from the top, cut out the lid on an angle. This way it won't drop inside the pumpkin when you put it back on top.

3. **Scoop out all the pulp** (and then some). An ice cream scoop works well. Thin the inner wall of the "face" area to 1¼ inch thick, so it will be easier to pierce the shell.

4. **Sketch out your design** on paper first. Tape it to the front of your pumpkin, and use a fork or pencil to poke holes along the carving lines.

5. **Hold the pumpkin** in your lap. It's easier to create features when the face is gazing up at you. For precise cuts, try a serrated kitchen knife, precision knife or small saw. Just don't cut on a slant — clean up-and-down slices look best.

6. **Start by making simple** rough cuts. If you get the big pieces of pumpkin out of the way first, you can go back and clean up the edges of your design later.

7. **Use your scraps creatively.** Make a tongue, pipe or hair accessories out of discarded pieces of pumpkin shell, for example.

PAINT MARBLED PUMPKINS
This quick DIY trick uses nail polish to create a cool effect.

1. Fill a plastic container with warm water. (Use one that you don't mind getting dirty or stained.)

2. One by one, pour different colors of nail polish onto the water. Try to pour as close to the surface as possible to make sure the nail polish floats.

3. Swirl colors together with a skewer to create a marbled effect.

4. Moving quickly, dip the part of the pumpkin you want painted into the nail-polish-and-water mixture.

5. Lift the pumpkin out of the water, and let excess nail polish drip off. Set pumpkin aside to dry completely.

Consider carving a variety of gourds.

SCAN ME!
DIY SPOOKY HALLOWEEN PUMPKINS 3 WAYS WITH LIA GRIFFITH

THANKSGIVING DINNER CHEAT SHEET

Take on Turkey Day like a pro! Our generous estimates will likely leave you with delicious Thanksgiving leftovers to enjoy when all that hard work is over.

DISH	8 PEOPLE	16 PEOPLE	24 PEOPLE
Whole Turkey	8 lbs	16 lbs	Two 12 to 14 lb whole turkeys, or one whole turkey and one breast equal to about 24 lbs total
Dry Mix Stuffing	8 oz	16 oz	24 oz
Potatoes	3 lbs, or six large	6 lbs, or 12 large	9 lbs, or 18 large
Sweet Potatoes	3 lbs, or three large	6 lbs, or six large	9 lbs, or nine large
Canned Cranberry Sauce	Two 16 oz cans	Three 16 oz cans	Four 16 oz can
Butternut Squash	$3\frac{1}{2}$ lbs, or two small	$9\frac{3}{4}$ lbs, or three medium	10 lbs, or four large
Brussels Sprouts	Two 10 oz containers	Four 10 oz containers	Six 10 oz containers
Green Beans	2 lbs	4 lbs	6 lbs
Frozen Creamed Spinach	Three 10 oz packages	Six 10 oz packages	Eight 10 oz packages
Pie	One to two, 9 to $9\frac{1}{2}$ inch	Two to three, 9 to $9\frac{1}{2}$ inch	Three to four, 9 to $9\frac{1}{2}$ inch

ROAST YOUR BEST TURKEY

We've cooked up more than 1,000 (!) turkeys over the years, so we've seen it all. Here's our favorite recipe.

Serves **12–14**
Total time: **3 hours, 20 minutes**

Heat oven to 375°F. Working on a baking sheet, remove the giblets and neck of a turkey (12–14 lbs), thawed if frozen, from its cavities. Reserve neck and discard giblets. Pat the turkey dry. Stuff 2 small onions and ¼ bunch of thyme into the main cavity. Tie the turkey legs together with kitchen twine. Tuck the wing tips underneath the body (this will prevent them from burning). Rub the turkey

with 3 Tbsp. softened butter or olive oil and season with ½ tsp. each Kosher salt and pepper. Place the turkey neck, 2 large carrots (cut into 2-inch pieces), 2 stalks of celery (cut into 2-inch pieces), 2 small onions and 8 sprigs of thyme (or more if you like) in a large roasting pan. Place a roasting rack in the pan, and place the turkey on top. Roast the turkey until a thermometer inserted into the thickest part of the thigh registers 165°F, 2½ to 3 hr. (Cover the turkey loosely with foil

if it browns too quickly, and add ¾ cup low-sodium chicken broth to the pan if the vegetables begin to scorch.) Carefully tilt the turkey to empty the juices from its cavity into the pan. Transfer the turkey to a carving board or cutting board set in a rimmed baking sheet (to catch juices while carving). Cover loosely with foil and let rest at least 30 min. Reserve the pan and its contents to make gravy (see page 198). Carve and garnish the turkey as desired.

Carve Your Bird

Our foolproof turkey-carving method is as follows:

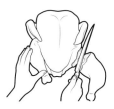   

1 Discard the twine (if you used any to tie up the turkey). Then remove the legs. Cut down in between where the leg meets the breast to remove the entire leg. Transfer to another cutting board. Repeat with the other leg.

2 Remove the breast and the wing. Cut along one side of the breastbone and, using the non-knife hand, gently pull the breast meat away from the bone. Cut as closely to the bone and ribs as possible, and then cut through the wing joint. Transfer to the other cutting board.

3 Separate the drumsticks from the thighs. Transfer the drumsticks to a platter. Remove the thigh bones, then slice the thigh meat and transfer to the platter. Remove the wings from the breasts and transfer to the platter, if your family and guests like the wings.

4 Slice the turkey breast crosswise (against the grain) and arrange on the platter.

LAB TIP If you're buying a whole turkey, plan on 1 lb (uncooked) per person. For a boneless turkey breast, get $1/2$ lb per person. Feeding an army? Rather than buying the biggest bird you can find (which can be tricky to cook evenly while retaining moisture), get two smaller turkeys or one whole turkey and one breast.

Prepare Great Sides

Thyme-Roasted Turkey Gravy

Makes **3 ¹/₂ cups**
Total time: **25 minutes**

Remove and discard the vegetables, thyme and neck from the roasting pan. Strain the pan drippings into a measuring cup; let stand 5 min. so the fat rises to the top. Spoon off the fat and pour the juices into a large (4-cup) measuring cup.

Place the empty roasting pan across two stove burners on medium-high. Add 1 cup dry white wine and cook, stirring and scraping up any browned bits, 1 min. Pour the wine mixture into the measuring cup with the pan juices and add enough low-sodium chicken broth (about 2 cups) to make 4 cups liquid total.

Melt 4 Tbsp. unsalted butter in a large saucepan on medium. Sprinkle ¹/₃ cup all-purpose flour over the top and cook, whisking, until deep brown, 4 to 5 min. Gradually whisk in the broth mixture; bring to a boil. Add 4 sprigs of fresh thyme, reduce heat and simmer, stirring occasionally, until thickened, 8 to 12 min. Season with salt and pepper. Strain just before serving.

Delectable Green Beans

Serves **4**
Total time: **30 minutes**

Heat 1 tsp. olive oil in a medium saucepan on medium. Add 1 shallot, finely chopped, and cook until tender, 4 to 5 min. Add 1¹/₂ cups dry sherry wine, ¹/₂ cup sherry vinegar and 2 Tbsp. brown sugar, and simmer until syrupy and reduced by three-quarters, 15 to 20 min. Whisk in 1 Tbsp. cold unsalted butter, then toss with 1 lb green beans, blanched, and ¹/₂ tsp. each salt and pepper.

LAB TIP Stuffing baked outside the bird, in a deep casserole dish, is the safest (and tastiest!) option.

Super Stuffing

Makes **5 cups**
Total time: **1 hour**

Heat oven to 375°F. Grease a 3-quart casserole dish. Heat 3 Tbsp. unsalted butter in a 12-inch skillet on medium. Add 2 medium onions, chopped, 1 tsp. kosher salt and ¹/₂ tsp. pepper and cook, covered, stirring occasionally, until very tender and beginning to turn golden, 6 to 8 min. Add 2 stalks of celery, chopped, and cook, stirring occasionally, until tender, 6 to 7 min. Add 3 cups low-sodium chicken broth and bring to a boil. Stir in ¹/₄ cup sage leaves, chopped, and cook 1 min. Remove from heat and stir in 1 cup flat-leaf parsley, chopped.

Transfer the vegetable mixture to a large bowl with about 10 cups cubed, toasted bread; toss to combine. Fold in 2 large eggs, beaten. Transfer to the prepared baking dish, cover with foil and bake 10 min. Remove foil and bake until golden brown, 15 to 20 min.

MAKE a WREATH for ANY OCCASION

Purchase a wreath mold or foam form from a craft store, then use our ideas to decorate your front door.

Halloween Wreath

Create a spooky display with an assortment of plastic snakes wrapped onto a wreath form covered with twigs. Start with the largest snakes you have and intertwine them between the twigs, repeating until you use all your rubber snakes and cover as many twigs as you can. Use hot glue as needed to hold them to the wreath.

SCAN ME!
WREATH MAKING 101

Handkerchief Wreath

Find dozens of handkerchiefs or fabric swatches in coordinating colors — some plain, some patterned — and weave or tie them around a wire wreath form.

Ruffly Ribbon Wreath

Cover a foam wreath in bows. Use pins to secure the bows.

Sweet Heart Wreath

Glue on overlapping hearts in different sizes to spread a little love.

Deck the Halls Wreath

Attach colorful ornaments to a faux wreath. Warm shades, such as pink, red, orange, yellow and gold, go on one side; cool tones, such as blue, purple, green and silver go on the other.

Bountiful Flower Wreath

Weave artificial flowers on a mold for a timeless option that you can enjoy year after year.

Wintry Snow Wreath

Round up sticks, twigs and pinecones from your backyard, and adhere them to a foam wreath. For a snow-covered effect, apply a light coat of white spray paint.

BAKE the BEST HOLIDAY COOKIES

Use our basic sugar dough to make a season's worth of treats.

Makes **36 to 48** (depending on cookie cutter size and shape)
Total time: **25 minutes, plus chilling and cooling**

1 In a large bowl, whisk together 2¾ cups all-purpose flour, ½ tsp. baking powder and ½ tsp. salt; set aside.

2 Using an electric mixer, beat 1 cup (2 sticks) unsalted butter, at room temperature, and ¾ cup granulated sugar in another large bowl on medium speed until light and fluffy, about 3 min. Beat in 1 large egg and then 1½ tsp. pure vanilla extract.

3 Reduce the mixer speed to low and gradually add flour mixture, mixing just until incorporated.

4 Shape the dough into three disks and roll each between two sheets of parchment paper to ⅛ to ¼ inch thick. Chill until firm, 30 min. in the refrigerator or 15 min. in the freezer.

5 Heat oven to 350°F. Line two baking sheets with parchment paper. Using floured cookie cutters, cut out cookies and place them onto the prepared sheets, spacing them 2 inches apart. Reroll, chill, and cut the scraps.

6 Bake, rotating the positions of the baking sheets halfway through, until the cookies are lightly golden brown around the edges, 10 to 12 min. Let cool on the baking sheets for 5 min., then transfer to wire racks to cool completely.

Decorator's Icing

In a bowl, with the mixer on medium speed, beat 16 oz confectioners' sugar, 3 Tbsp. meringue powder and ⅓ cup warm water until blended and mixture is very stiff, about 5 min. Makes 3 cups.

LAB TIP Tint icing with food coloring as desired; press plastic wrap directly onto surface to prevent it from drying out. For piping, thin icing slightly with water. Spoon into decorating bags to decorate cooled cookies.

Choco-Dipped Trees

Cut into trees. When cool, dip half of each tree in melted dark chocolate and sprinkle with multicolored sanding sugar.

Glazed Holly Hearts

Cut into hearts. When cool, decorate with red, green and white icing.

Crunchy Candy Canes

Cut into candy cane shapes. When cool, drizzle with white chocolate and sprinkle with crushed peppermints.

Sparkling Wreaths

Cut into wreaths. When cool, decorate with green icing and press into green sanding sugar. With dab of icing, affix 3 mini M&M's to each.

Sprinkle Mittens

Cut into mittens. When cool, decorate with icing, colored sprinkles and mini marshmallows.

Holiday Snickerdoodles

Instead of cutting the dough, scoop and roll into 1-inch balls in a small bowl of cinnamon sugar; place on a cookie sheet. Pat to flatten slightly.

Peppermint Drops

Instead of cutting the dough, scoop and roll into 1-inch balls; place on a cookie sheet. Pat to flatten. After removing the cookies from the oven, immediately press a peppermint candy kiss into the center of each cookie.

Stained-Glass "Ornaments"

Cut into ornaments. With smaller cutters, cut out the centers. With a straw, cut a small hole at the top of each for a ribbon. Bake cookies 7 min., then fill each decorative hole with ¼ to ½ tsp. crushed hard candies. Bake another 3 to 5 min. After cookies cool, thread ribbon through the holes at the tops.

Candy Cane Wands

Before dividing the dough, remove half the dough from the mixing bowl. Beat in red food coloring and ½ tsp. peppermint extract. Scoop and shape into 2-inch-long strands. Twist two strands together, one of each color.

SCAN ME!
COOL USES FOR COOKIE CUTTERS

FIND the PERFECT TREE

Don't know your white spruce from your balsam fir? Not to worry! Here's our rundown of the different types of Christmas trees and tips on what will work best for you.

Balsam Fir

If what you want most is the it-must-be-Christmas smell when you walk in the door, opt for a balsam fir, thought to be the most fragrant of the Christmas tree varieties. Its conical shape and dark green colors are also quintessentially on message. Another plus is this tree's great needle retention.

Colorado Blue Spruce

The appeal of the Colorado blue spruce is, as its name suggests, its blue/silvery appearance, perfect for a wintry living room. This tree's rigid branches tend to have sharp needles, which might help keep pets away, if yours tend to be curious.

Douglas Fir

Douglas firs are popular because of their perfect pyramid shape. Also, since they radiate dark-green or blue-green needles in all directions, Douglas firs are usually nice and full. These soft needles (and the rest of the tree) need a lot of water.

Eastern Red Cedar

With needles that jet straight upward, eastern red cedars are particularly dense and green. Fun fact: Despite its name, it's not actually a cedar tree — it's really a part of the juniper family.

Eastern White Pine

These are best if you're going for a natural look and want the tree to be the focus in and of itself; according to the National Christmas Tree Association, the eastern white pine's soft, flexible branches aren't great for hefty ornaments.

Fraser Fir

For those who like to go all out with decorations, the Fraser fir might be the best bet, thanks to stiff branches and soft needles. Speaking of needles, this tree has great needle retention and a lovely evergreen smell.

White Fir

Also called the concolor fir, this tree has been gaining in popularity, no doubt due to its bluish-green-silver color and citrusy aroma. This tree also boasts excellent needle retention.

White Spruce

The National Christmas Tree Association says the white spruce is wonderful for ornaments because of the tree's short, stiff bluish-green needles.

LAB TIP Got an awkwardly shaped present? There's a box for that! Once you've placed it in a box (and, if necessary, protected the gift by layering in tissue paper, wrapping it in bubble wrap or gently scrunching up kraft paper), follow our steps on the next page.

WRAP ANY SIZE BOX

Taking the time to wrap a gift with handsome paper, ribbons and bows is another way to show the recipient just how much you care. Our step-by-step tutorial will show you exactly how to do it.

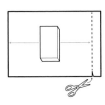 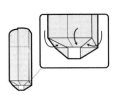 

1 Measure and cut the wrapping paper. Before cutting, place the box facedown on the wrapping paper to gauge how much you need to completely cover all sides. Cut the gift wrap along one side.

2 Fold over the wrapping paper. After making sure that the box is centered on the paper, pull the paper tautly up and over one side until it reaches the center of the box. Secure with double-sided tape.

3 Join the ends of the wrapping paper. Bring the other end of the paper up and over to meet the taped side. For a cleaner look, fold at least a half-inch of wrapping paper under, using your fingernail to create a sharp crease. Secure the paper with double-sided tape.

4 Tape the open ends on both sides. If the ends of the wrapping paper are too long for your box, trim them down. One end at a time, create 45-degree angle flaps with a "push in, crease, push in, crease" method. Pull paper taut before fastening with tape. Repeat on the other side of the box.

5 Add finishing touches like bows, ribbons and gift labels. Double up on ribbon in contrasting shades, and curl it with scissors for a finished look.

SUPPLIES
- Wrapping paper
- Double-sided tape
- Scissors
- Ribbon, bows, gift tags

SCAN ME!
GENIUS TOOLS TO MAKE GIFT WRAPPING EASIER

WRITE the PERFECT HOLIDAY CARD

If you find yourself with a case of holiday card writer's block, remember to keep your message short and simple. Summarize a few positive life events — no boasting or embellishing — and follow with a line or two of genuine best wishes. Our suggestions will help you get started writing thoughtful notes for all the special people in your life.

General

- "May your holidays sparkle with joy and laughter."

- "I hope the magic of the holidays fills every corner of your heart and home with joy — now and always."

- "May your family have a holiday season that is full of wonderful surprises, treats and nonstop laughter."

- "Happy holidays! I hope all your Christmas wishes come true."

Funny

- "Merry everything! May your joy be large and your bills small."

- "This holiday season, let's make it a point to cherish what's truly important in our lives: cookies."

- "I told Santa you were good this year and sent him a link to your Pinterest board. Merry Christmas to you!"

- "This Christmas, may your family be functional and all your batteries included."

For Faraway Friends

- "I wish we could be together this holiday season, but I'm sending warm wishes your way."

- "I'll miss celebrating with you this season. Eat a few cookies for me."

- "Even though we're apart, our hearts are together."

- "Missing you most during this festive time."

For Hard Holidays

- "Wishing you love and light in this challenging season."

- "Our hearts are with you and yours."

- "We know you might be having a difficult time this year, more than ever. Wishing you strength and peace in these trying times."

- "Sometimes the holidays remind us of what we've lost. Remember that I'm always there for you."

Propose a New Year's Toast

Sure, you don't need to make a New Year's toast before you clink glasses. But doing so makes the night more memorable — and will help get the party started and the champagne flowing. These toasts are short and sweet and easy to memorize ahead of the party.

- "Here's to a bright New Year and a fond farewell to the old; here's to the things that are yet to come and to the memories that we hold."

- "Out with the old, in with the new, cheers to the future, and all that we do."

- "May all your troubles during the coming year be as short as your New Year's resolutions."

- "Here's a toast to the future, a toast to the past, and a toast to our friends, far and near."

- "Wishing you more happiness than all my words can tell."

- "To those who've seen us at our best and at our worst and can't tell the difference."

TRANSFORM YOUR TABLE

The centerpiece is the focal point of your table, so give your guests something fun to look at. Lovely flowers always add a festive touch (see page 107 for tips on easy arrangements), or you can try one of these suggestions for a little DIY flair.

Layer moss and LED lights in a mason jar to mimic fireflies.

Display a collection of clean bottles. Use old or antique ones for a charming, rustic display, or newer ones for a sleeker look (soak off labels or stickers). Trim stems to the height you'd like, then insert a blossom in each bottle.

Decorate fruit — pears, grapes, apples, you name it — with a dusting of artificial snow, glittery or otherwise, for a magical holiday centerpiece.

Shake up a can of gold spray paint, and use it to transform twigs, branches, leaves, pinecones and fruit.

Highlight uncommon items with interesting textures, then build a theme around them. Think spools of thick yarn, knitting needles, and knit textiles for a cozy affair.

Fill the center of the table with candles of different heights. Maximize the glow by placing the candles on a mirror.

Pick up a bunch of apothecary jars and stuff them with lavender, moss and twigs for a more natural look.

SET a FORMAL TABLE

Proper place settings might seem fussy, but there's a reason for the time-tested blueprint — it follows the logical progression of the meal and makes dining more comfortable for your guests. Here's how to get it right:

Bread Plate
Butter knife handle faces right for easy reach.

Dessert Fork and Spoon
Tuck in dessert utensils above the plate — fork handle left, spoon handle right.

Utensils
Forks on the left; knives (blades in) and spoons on the right. Everything is placed from the outside in based on course order — for instance, set for soup, salad and then entrée.

Glasses
Water is placed above knives for easy access. If you're serving both red and white wine, set glasses right to left in the order used: White wine for the first course on the outside, then red next for your entrée.

ORIGAMI NAPKIN FOLDS

Take your tablescape from ordinary to conversation-worthy in minutes.

UTENSIL POCKET
Fold a square napkin in half, then into quarters to make a smaller square. Bring one open corner down to the opposite corner. Turn the napkin over and fold into thirds by bringing the two sides inward. Turn over to reveal an elegant pocket for cutlery.

BOW
Here's a simple yet stunning way to dress up your dining room for sit-down gatherings. It couldn't be quicker — just wrap each place setting with a length of wide, pretty ribbon.

BE a GOOD GUEST

Being a thoughtful and considerate guest will all but guarantee a return invitation.

RSVP.
Respond sooner rather than later so you won't forget — and so your host can plan accordingly.

Come bearing a gift.
Bringing a trinket of appreciation, flowers, a bottle of wine or some baked goods (check out our advice for gift giving on page 214) is a gracious way of saying thank-you.

Give hosts a head's up.
Let your host know about any food allergies or sensitivities before you arrive. Waiting until the day of might throw off someone's menu or meal-prep.

Ask before bringing a guest.
Or your kids. Or your pet. Don't assume anyone else is automatically invited, no matter how well you know your host.

Follow the house rules.
For example, if shoes are left at the front door, take yours off without complaint.

Fess up to a spill immediately.
The longer it sets, the harder it might be to clean. Offer to pay for any professional services that might be required.

Greet everyone when you enter a room.
If you don't personally know someone at a party or gathering, it's polite to say a quick hello and introduce yourself.

Learn people's names.
Memorizing someone's name and using it is a sign of respect.

BE a GREAT CONVERSATIONALIST

Like making a terrific turkey or hanging a gallery wall, having a sparkling conversation is a skill that can absolutely be learned.

Look at the person speaking to you. It's impolite to be glancing down at your phone while someone is talking to you. Eye contact signals that you're listening.

Come prepared with ice-breaker questions if you're nervous about initiating a conversation: What was the first concert you went to? How would you spend a million dollars? If you could have any animal for a pet, what would it be and why? What's one thing you're better at than anyone else?

Focus on similarities. Somehow you and the person you're talking to wound up at this same party or event. Ask the person how they know the host. It's basic, but it beats talking about the weather.

Listen. The more actively you listen to the person, the likelier it is that you'll have natural follow-up questions or comments to make, and the more the conversation will flow.

Stay positive. Avoid negative, or potentially negative, subjects with someone you've just met. Keep it light and fun. Even if you head into serious territory, try not to be overly critical, judgmental or hyperbolic.

Be empathetic. Remember that people get passionate about things that are close to them, often for very personal and sometimes private reasons. Try to see the other person's position from a place of empathy, sensitivity and understanding.

Rehearse beforehand. If you know you'll be encountering someone with whom you've clashed in the past, practice a few innocuous statements like "Let's agree to disagree" or "I know we don't see eye to eye on this topic, but I bet we can agree that [insert host's name] throws an awesome party, right?"

Aim to spend between $15 and $50 — anything less seems cheap, and anything more seems too luxurious.

Steer clear of decor, including art, unless you're absolutely sure about the person's taste.

Rewrap any regifts. To ensure that the original gift didn't contain a personal note to you, open it, search it thoroughly and carefully rewrap it.

Choose nut-free foods. If you don't know your host and the possible allergies in their house, avoid anything with nuts. You can't go wrong with chocolate, a flowering plant or a bottle of wine.

Send a gift the day after if it would be awkward for the host to keep track of during the event. If you're going to a party that's not at someone's home, remember that your host will need to carry or keep track of whatever you bring. It's also important to avoid anything that will need tending to right away, like a large bouquet of flowers that requires arranging in water.

BRING a THOUGHTFUL GIFT

It's a charming rule to follow: Never arrive empty handed. Here are some good ideas to pick the perfect present for your host.

WRITE the NICEST THANK-YOU NOTE

Emails and texts are wonderful, but nothing beats a thoughtful card sent post-event or -visit. Keep a few blank cards on hand, so you'll be able to share your thanks as soon as you get home.

1 Be thoughtful in your greeting. Include a salutation and use the person's first name (unless you don't know each other well).

2 Radiate friendliness. Use your natural voice and write as if you're speaking with the recipient — a casual tone will come across as more genuine.

3 Use specific examples. Mention the gift or act of kindness specifically and describe how you'll use it or what the favor or present meant to you.

4 Sign smartly. Close in a way that reflects your relationship: "Love" for family or good friends; "Fondly" for people you know fairly well; "Sincerely" for acquaintances.

INDEX

PHOTOGRAPHY CREDITS

Cover: Mike Garten

Amber Ulmer: 140; **Andrew Beasley:** 87; **Annie Schlechter:** 66; **Antonis Achilleos:** 193; **Beatriz Da Costa:** 58; **Buff Strickland:** 96; **David Hillegas:** 201; **David Tsay:** 71; **Emily Kate Roemer:** 201; **Erika LaPresto:** 4, 55; **Jane Beiles:** 118; **Jens Mortensen:** 180; **John Kernick:** 192; **Jonny Valiant:** 88; **José David:** 140; **Kat Teutsch:** 168; **Mark Scott:** 78, 82, 86, 96; **Philip Ficks:** 36; **Tara Donne:** 80; **Tessa Neustadt:** 140

Brian Woodcock: 2, 83, 96, 103, 150, 162, 169, 201, 210

Brown Bird Design (icons and illustrations): 1, 11, 12, 13, 23, 24, 26, 57, 67, 75, 91, 92, 94, 106, 115, 127, 130, 146, 158, 197, 207, 212

Danielle Daly: 22, 86, 100, 101, 137, 188, 189, 206

Getty Images: 6, 15, 16, 20, 21, 29, 31, 32, 33, 35, 39, 45, 46, 51, 52, 53. 56, 73, 74, 93, 95, 96, 104, 105, 107, 108, 109, 110, 112, 114, 117, 124, 126, 131, 133, 134, 136, 138, 144, 147, 148, 152, 154, 155, 156, 159, 163, 170, 172, 174, 176, 182, 183, 184, 186, 201, 204, 205, 209, 213, 214, 215

Mike Garten: 8, 10, 25, 26, 27, 28, 30, 31, 37, 41, 42, 44, 48, 61, 62, 65, 72, 76, 81, 84, 90, 99, 111, 121, 140, 143, 153, 160, 164, 171, 179, 180, 181, 187, 190, 193, 195, 196, 199, 200, 201, 202, 203, 222, 224

Noun Project (icons and illustrations): 14, 15, 17, 18, 19, 34, 38, 39, 54, 56, 59, 60, 63, 65, 68, 69, 72, 85, 97, 102, 122, 123, 125, 128, 129, 133, 173, 178, 189, 201, 203, 207, 208

Back Cover: Mike Garten and Getty Images

LAB TIP Matching baskets will look uniform even if their shapes and sizes are different. For more tips to beautify your bathroom see page 82.

Cover and book design by Miguel Rivera

Library of Congress Cataloging-in-Publication Data Available on request

10 9 8 7 6 5 4 3 2 1

Published by Hearst Home, an imprint of Hearst Books/Hearst Communications, Inc.
300 W 57th Street
New York, NY 10019

Good Housekeeping, Hearst Home, the Hearst Home logo, and Hearst Books are registered trademarks of Hearst Communications, Inc.

For information about custom editions, special sales, premium and corporate purchases:
hearst.com/magazines/hearst-books

Printed in Canada

ISBN 978-1-950785-20-9

LAB TIP When harvesting from your herb garden, pick a mixture of leaves — old, new, large, small — to ensure continued growth. For more tips see page 108.